101 BEST TV CRIME SERIES

Other books by Mark Timlin

A Good Year for the Roses 1988

Romeo's Tune 1990

Gun Street Girl 1990

Take the A-Train 1991

The Turnaround 1992

Hearts of Stone 1992

Zip Gun Boogie 1992

Falls the Shadow 1993

Ashes by Now 1993

Pretend We're Dead 1994

Paint It Black 1995

Find My Way Home 1996

Sharman and Other Filth (short stories) 1996

A Street That Rhymed at 3 AM 1997

Dead Flowers 1998

Quick Before They Catch Us 1999

All the Empty Places 2000

Stay Another Day 2010

OTHERS

I Spied a Pale Horse 1999

Answers from the Grave 2004

Guns of Brixton 2010

as TONY WILLIAMS

Valin's Raiders 1994

Blue on Blue 1999

as JIM BALLANTYNE

The Torturer 1995

as MARTIN MILK

That Saturday 1996

as LEE MARTIN

Gangsters Wives 2007

The Lipstick Killers 2009

101 BEST
TV CRIME SERIES

Bad Guys, Spies & Private Eyes

MARK TIMLIN

No Exit Press

First published in 2010 by No Exit Press,
an imprint of Oldcastle Books Ltd,
PO Box 394, Harpenden, Herts, AL5 1XJ

www.noexit.co.uk

ISBN 978-1-84243-350-8

2 4 6 8 10 9 7 5 3 1

Typeset by JC Services, Ealing, London W5 1NX

Printed and bound in Great Britain by J F Print Ltd., Sparkford, Somerset

For Nick David

ABOUT THE AUTHOR

Mark Timlin is the creator of South London's premier private detective, Nick Sharman. Born in Cheltenham, Gloucestershire on 15th June 1944 (at the local borstal requisitioned by the Royal Navy for the use of the WRNS as a maternity home), within nine days he was back in London with his mother and grandmother dodging V2 rockets, and spending most days under the kitchen table in the family's Kilburn home. When Timlin was seven, the family relocated to Tulse Hill in South London where he was later educated at the Strand Grammar School in nearby Brixton Hill. As a young adult, Timlin tried various jobs: a forklift truck driver, mini cab driver, skateboard manufacturer, roadie for T-Rex and The Who (giving him a healthy sampling of the excesses of the era – which he was later to put to good fictional use). It wasn't until 1985, faced with another period on the dole, that Timlin decided to add 'novelist' to his ever expanding CV.

A Good Year For The Roses (1988) was Timlin's answer to the hardboiled noir of 1940s America, uprooted lock, stock and barrel to the dingy back streets of 1980s South London. Nick Sharman, a down-at-heel ex-copper with a gunshot wound in his foot, is opening his own private investigation business in a shop front close to Tulse Hill station when he is hired to track down a teenage runaway named Patsy Bright.

Timlin's love of vintage cars is reflected in the vehicle that Sharman drives – a shiny E-Type Jaguar, which comes to a sticky end during a particularly frenetic car chase. Combining humour with brutal violence, Timlin's breezy writing style tapped into the rich tradition of British gangster films such as *Get Carter* (1971) and *The Long Good Friday* (1980) with Sharman himself very much a modern take on the quintessentially American Philip Marlowe-style 'tec, which mirrors the author's love of Raymond Chandler, Ross McDonald,

Richard Stark, John D. McDonald et al. More Sharman books followed, with *The Turnaround* (1991) being chosen to launch Sharman's television career in a one-off pilot starring Clive Owen. Alas, caught in the crossfire of media hysteria concerning screen violence following the tragic Dunblane massacre in March 1996, the series proper was eventually shunted to a late time slot, only managing four more episodes before the plug was pulled. Latterly though, it has enjoyed re-showings, a DVD release and a welcome reappraisal.

Other notable Sharman books include *Pretend We're Dead* (1994) and *Quick Before They Catch Us* (1999) which dealt with the hot topic of racism in the Asian community, in both London and Manchester. *All The Empty Places* (2000) saw Sharman dealing with the problems of a girlfriend, when a thuggish ex-flame of hers promised violent retribution, and had the surprising plot turn of Sharman leaving the country to live on a Caribbean island. After a long break *Stay Another Day* (2009) sees the return of Sharman to London when his daughter is in danger.

Answers From The Grave (2004 aka *Guns of Brixton*) is a long (for Timlin) stand-alone novel about a criminal family in South London where Sharman makes a guest appearance. Timlin's nom-de-plumes include Jim Ballantyne, Martin Milk, Tony Williams and (most recently) Lee Martin for his more mainstream novel *Gangsters' Wives* (2007). This may have explored the female side of gangland violence, but it still offered the same copious amounts of sex and violence so prodigiously displayed in the author's previous more male-dominated offerings.

Timlin lives in Docklands, where he likes to keep a close eye on his South London roots, and is the crime critic for *The Independent on Sunday*.

Mark Campbell

Originally published in *British Crime Writing: An Ecyclopaedia* published by Greenwood World Publishing and reproduced by kind permission.

101 Best TV Crime Series

INTRODUCTION

So here it is. My first ever book of lists. And what a way to start, with my favourite TV genre-cop shows, incorporating *Bad Guys, Spies and Private Eyes*. And that ain't all. Within these 101 choices are all manner of heroes and villains, and some of the characters are both. But do remember one thing: this is *my* list of *my* favourite TV crime shows, so before anyone starts sharpening their long knives, if you don't agree with my choices, tough. I'm not interested, and if you do disagree, my advice is to do your own book. Or go to **www.crimeseries.tv** where you can sound off about your own favourite TV crime shows. Then find someone to publish it. I did. Anyway, this book is supposed to be fun, not a thesis for a university degree, so if you *do* disagree with my choices, as Mark Twain famously once said 'That's what makes horse races.'

Right. Now that's over and done with, let's set out some parameters. Simple. I've included any crime show that I have enjoyed since I was a nipper, and the TV had only two black and white channels; and maybe one or two even before that. And it's amazing, that, whilst researching this book, what memories a television programme can bring back. A bit like a song. And in fact, a lot of these shows are best remembered by their theme tunes. Some were even massive hits. And one or two spawned spin-off records that became popular too. *What Are We Gonna Get 'er Indoors For Christmas* by Dennis Waterman and George Cole springs to mind. There's no accounting for taste. And talking of research, particular thanks go to Nick David to whom this book is dedicated, and who scoured the internet for the price of a lunch at Roast restaurant in Borough Market, and who also tracked down DVDs of some of the more elusive shows from God knows where. And special thanks to Sophie Barnes at No Exit Press who went beyond the call of duty to source the internet addresses you'll find at the end of each item and check out the availability of each on DVD. Finally a shout up to Claire Watts and Ion Mills also at No Exit for getting the whole thing started and finished. All these programmes are in English, and the information is correct as I write (latter part of 2010) and any mistakes are my own. If the show is current I've given a rough idea of the number of episodes made, and when the show has been cancelled I've done my best to round up all known information. Anyway, enough of that for now. Join me in the world of DVD box sets, downloads, and afternoons in front of obscure satellite channels running repeats of series that no one watched in the first place. I hope you enjoy reading it as much as I enjoyed writing it. So where to start?

Well number one hundred is as good a place as any.

All programme titles with an asterisk after them have an entry of their own in this book

For a **FREE** ebook version of *101 Best TV Crime Series* visit:

www.crimeseries.tv

100. DEPARTMENT S / JASON KING

UK – ITV (Three Seasons)

Cast: Peter Wyngarde *(Jason King)*, Joel Fabiani *(Stewart Sullivan)*, Rosemary Nicols *(Annabelle Hurst)*, Dennis Alaba Peters *(Sir Curtis Seretse)*

Writers: Philip Broadley & Monty Berman

Producer: Monty Berman

First Broadcast (UK): Department S: 9 March 1969 – 4 March 1970

Jason King: 15 September 1971 – 28 April 1972

Runtime: 54 episodes x 60min

DVD: Network 2008

Department S is based in Paris. Nice work if you can get it and its speciality is solving cases that the might of Interpol cannot. That's all right then. Top man is Jason King, crime writer and ladies' man (more about that later), who reports to his guv'nor Sir Curtis Seretse (Dennis Alaba Peters). King's assignment is to imagine what his fictional detective character Mark Caine (Mark of Caine: you got to love it) would make of it. Not much, if you go by the brief passages King reads of his masterpieces. His partners in crime solving are Stewart Sullivan (Joel Fabiani) and Annabelle Hurst (Rosemary Nicols) to give (as they used to say) something for the dads to look at. A bit like Pan's People in *Top of the Pops:* apropos of nothing. The cases that the team took on were always of a bizarre nature, but fear not, our trusty cops never failed.

A year after the series finished Wyngarde returned in his own series called *Jason King* wearing even more flamboyant facial hair, shirt and tie combos, and suits so sharp they almost cut him. In Australia he was voted the man most women would like to lose their virginity to, but unfortunately a million female hearts were broken when an incident in a Gloucester public convenience hit the headlines. After that Wyngarde's career hit the skids and both he and Jason vanished into TV obscurity.

weblinks

www.imdb.com/title/tt0063893/
www.imdb.com/title/tt0066672/

www.tv.com/department-s/show/1194/summary.html?
en.wikipedia.org/wiki/Department_S
en.wikipedia.org/wiki/Jason_King_%28TV_series%29
www.amazon.co.uk/Department-S-1-2-Complete-DVD/dp/B0015B04I6/

99. ULTIMATE FORCE

UK – ITV (Four Seasons)
Cast: Miles Anderson *(Colonel Aidan Dempsey)*, Jamie Bamber
(Lt Dotsy Doheny), Ross Kemp *(Henry 'Henno' Garvie)*, Heather Peace
(Becca Gallagher)
Writers: Len Collin & Rob Heyland
Producers: Ian Strachan & Brian True-May
First Broadcast (UK): 16 September 2002 – 1 June 2008
Runtime: 11 episodes x 50min, 8 episodes x 70min, 1 episode x 74min,
1 episode x 94min
DVD: ITV Studios Home Entertainment 2008

Similar in plot to *The Unit* in the USA, *Ultimate Force* features a section of
the SAS who go where others fear to tread. Led by Colonel Aidan Dempsey
(Miles Anderson) and Lieutenant 'Dotsy' Doheny (Jamie Bamber) known as
Henry's by the real leader of Red Troop, chubby cheeked, ex-publican of The
Queen Vic in Albert Square, let's hear it for Sergeant 'Henno' Garvey played
by Ross Kemp. And by gum, these chaps don't pull any punches. When they
go in, the villains don't last long. Heavily armed and extremely dangerous
(including the token woman, Becca Gallagher played by Heather Peace)
nothing stops these warriors taking the high ground and winning the day.

weblinks

www.imdb.com/title/tt0334874/
en.wikipedia.org/wiki/Ultimate_Force
www.tv.com/ultimate-force/show/14335/summary.html?
www.amazon.co.uk/Ultimate-Force-Complete-Jamie-Draven/dp/B001CWLFJU/

98. NCIS

US – CH5 (Seven Seasons)
Cast: Mark Harmon *(Leroy Jethro Gibbs)*, Michael Weatherly
(Anthony DiNozzo), David McCallum *(Dr Donald Mallard)*, Pauley Perrette
(Abby Sciuto), Sean Murray *(Timothy McGee)*, Cote de Pablo *(Ziva David)*,
Brian Dietzen *(Jimmy Palmer)*
Writers: Donald P. Bellisario & Don McGill
Producers: Mark Horowitz, Donald P. Bellisario & Charles Floyd Johnson
First Broadcast (US): 23 September 2003 – Present
Runtime: 160 plus episodes x 60min
DVD: Paramount Home Entertainment 2010

Standing for Naval Criminal Investigative Service, NCIS stars Mark Harmon as Special Agent Leroy Jethro Gibbs, a grumpy, coffee-swilling, too often married Federal cop, who leads a crew of super investigators, including Special Agent Anthony Di Nozzo, played by Michael Weatherly as the only comedy type cop I can bear to watch, Pauley Perrette as a punk scientist who wears the most extraordinary clothes, and good old David McCallum, sexy Illya in *The Man From U.N.C.L.E.** as comfy Dr Donald 'Ducky' Mallard. As is obvious by the title, the team only investigate naval related crimes, ranging from theft of supplies, right up to murder.

This year, a spin-off series *NCIS Los Angeles* has appeared, featuring Chris O'Donnell and LL Cool J amongst others, but I must confess I've never seen it (Christ, I can't see everything, and new shows seem to arrive daily), but online crits have not been kind.

weblinks

www.imdb.com/title/tt0364845/
en.wikipedia.org/wiki/NCIS_%28TV_series%29
fxuk.com/shows/ncis
www.cbs.com/primetime/ncis/
www.amazon.co.uk/NCIS-Criminal-Investigative-Service-Complete/dp/B0036QV8LA/

** All programme titles with an asterix after them
have an entry of their own in this book*

97. THE MAN FROM U.N.C.L.E.

USA – BBC (Four Seasons)
Cast: Robert Vaughn *(Napoleon Solo),* David McCallum *(Illya Kuryakin),*
Leo G. Carroll *(Alexander Waverly)*
Writers: Dean Hargrove & Peter Allan Fields
Producers: Norman Felton
First Broadcast (US): 24 June 1965 – 15 January 1968
Runtime: 105 episodes x 50min; Black and White: Season 1;
Colour: Seasons 2 – 4
DVD: Warner Home Video 2003

The man from the United Network Command for Law and Enforcement
(Pretty clunky I think you'll agree, as the acronym was only given meaning
on the insistence of fans. Originally it was used because it sounded like
something from a James Bond movie. As a matter of fact, some experts
think it's 'Nations' not 'Network'. But that could be splitting hairs.), is
suave and sophisticated Napoleon Solo played by Robert Vaughan,
whose headquarters are hidden away behind the Del Floria tailor's shop
in Manhattan which is pretty handy when he needed alterations to his
razor sharp wool/mohair mix whistle and flutes, and whose boss is Mr
Alexander Waverly (Leo G. Carroll). The idea originated at a lunch between
the producer, Norman Felton and James Bond's own creator Ian Fleming.
I wouldn't mind having been at that lunch. Fleming came up with the
name Solo, which was a character in *Goldfinger*, and was originally to be
the title of the series, but, as often happens, more sober heads decreed
that Fleming drop out, and only the idea and one name remained. Solo
is assisted by Illya Kuryakin, a young Russian agent played to the hilt by
David McCallum. Although Vaughn was the star, it was McCallum that
really rocked the show to the top of the ratings. During the run of the
series, McCallum became a sex symbol, and even had a record dedicated
to him (*Love Ya Illya*, by *Angela & the Fans*, who was in fact Alma Cogan, a
very glamorous superstar of stage, variety and early TV, who was famed

for her over-the-top costumes, and rumours of naughty goings on at the parties she used to hold in her glamorous West End apartment. She was even supposed to have had a fling with John Lennon, although it was also rumoured that her proclivity was more with the distaff side. And before you ask, yes I do have a copy of the record). McCallum even made his own stab at the charts with several forgettable records of his own. (And I'll be the first to admit I've forgotten the titles. But thanks to Professor Eric White of Out Of Time Records in Norwich, I have the information. The single was called *Communication,* and two albums: *Music A Part Of Me (1966)* and *Music A Bit More Of Me (1967).* Pretentious? Not at all. His father actually played violin on *Sergeant Pepper.* Not many people know that.) Strange to think that, all these years later, McCallum is a TV star again, playing cuddly Donald 'Ducky' Mallard in *NCIS*,* about as far from a sex symbol as one could imagine.

U.N.C.L.E.'s (sometimes the full stops were dropped from the title. You pays your money and you takes your choice) bitter enemy was THRUSH (No explanation for that acronym, or full stops for that matter) an international mob of gangsters who mostly came out second to Solo and his pals.

Vaughn himself is now one of the ensemble actors in *Hustle*,* still as suave as hell, and the writer of a fascinating autobiography. The instantly recognisable theme was by Jerry Goldsmith.

Now here's an interesting footnote, talking of Alma Cogan. According to John L. William's biography of Shirley Bassey (*Miss Shirley Bassey,* Quercus 2010), sometime in 1962, her then husband Kenneth Hume made a pilot for a TV crime show called *The Secret Keepers* starring Cogan as a private eye, Frankie Howerd as a runaway husband she's trying to locate, and Bassey herself as a street busker. The mind bloody boggles. Apparently the show was completed, but never shown, although the *Daily Mail* ran a story about it illustrated with stills. Now that's one programme I'd dearly love to see.

96. THE LONG FIRM

UK – BBC2 (One Season)
Cast: Mark Strong *(Harry Starks)*, Derek Jacobi *(Teddy Thursby)*,
Phil Daniels *(Jimmy)*
Writers: Jake Arnott & Joe Penhall
Producers: David Bernath, Laura Mackie & Hilary Salmon
First Broadcast (UK): 7 July 2004 – 28 July 2004
Runtime: 4 episodes x 60min
DVD: BBC2 Entertain Video 2004

Adapted from the novel by Jake Arnott, which I didn't rate much, this four-part series was saved by the appearance of Mark Strong as Harry Starks, a vicious, homosexual thug who layered a thin veneer of respectability over his nasty self, as he plied his trade in 1960s London, moving effortlessly from the East to the West End. In fact, I nearly gave it a miss, until a friend gave me a heads up (doncha just hate that expression) and lent me a video of the first episode. After that I was hooked.

95. INSPECTOR GEORGE GENTLY

UK – BBC (Two Seasons)
Cast: Martin Shaw *(George Gently)*, Lee Ingleby *(John Bacchus)*,
Simon Hubbard *(PC Taylor)*
Writers: Peter Flannery & Alan Hunter
Producers: George Faber, Charles Pattinson, Peter Flannery,
Polly Hill & Andrew Lowe
First Broadcast (UK): 8 April 2007 – Present
Runtime: 9 episodes x 90min
DVD: Acorn Media 2009

When I joined the adult library in West Norwood aged twelve, the first crime novels I remember reading were the *Gently* series by Alan Hunter. I thought they were good at the time, and they were definitely *of* the time. The 1950s. As gentle as the hero's name and as comfortable as the old mac he always seemed to wear on the slipcover illustrations. I always thought they were set in East Anglia, so I wondered, when I saw the TV series, why they were relocated to Northumberland (I still do.) As a matter of fact, I almost didn't bother with the series as Martin Shaw, who plays Gently as a right grumpy old git with a very strange speaking voice, was awful in his last series, *Judge John Deed*. (Is it in his contract that programmes he stars in always have to have a Christian name in the title? Discuss. On second thought, don't bother.) Half the fun of watching dramas set in a period you have lived through is picking out the anomalies. (Actually this one is pretty good, unlike, say *Heartbeat*.) Lee Ingleby is excellent as Gently's sergeant, though I doubt his hair length would have passed muster at the time.

weblinks

www.imdb.com/title/tt1430509/
www.tv.com/inspector-george-gently/show/71793/summary.html?
en.wikipedia.org/wiki/Inspector_George_Gently
www.amazon.co.uk/George-Gently-BBC-Martin-Shaw/dp/B001CAR1WW/

94.   HAMISH MACBETH

UK – BBC1 (Three Seasons)
Cast: Robert Carlyle *(Hamish Macbeth)*, Ralph Riach *(TV John McIver)*,
Brian Pettifer *(Rory Campbell)*, Stuart Davids *(Lachie McCrae)*,
Anne Lacey *(Esme Murray)*
Writer: M C Beaton
Producers: Deirdre Keir & Charles Salmon
First Broadcast (UK): 26 March 1995 – 4 May 1997
Runtime: 20 episodes x 50 min
DVD: Cinema Club 2006

You may well ask why this gentle, Sunday evening on BBC1, fare is featured here next to more hard-boiled series. And I may well tell you. Firstly, there are few cop shows where the leading man openly smokes dope whilst on patrol. The police dog is no snarling Alsatian but a white West Highland Terrier named Wee Jock, until a sad hit-and-run accident, which squashed the poor young fellow and caused him to be replaced unsurprisingly with Wee Jock 2. Hamish, the cop himself, played straight-faced by Robert Carlyle, and as far away from his character in *Trainspotting* as is possible, helps poachers make off with the laird of Lochdubh's (pronounced Lochdoo and actually Plockton) salmon, takes part in late night sessions in the local pub, and positively supports a pirate radio station run by some of the village lads. The crimes Hamish investigates are many and strange. In fact, there seems to be a force field around the village rather as if it were a latter day Midwich, home of the cuckoos, or possibly Brigadoon, which only wakes up once every hundred years.

The series was based on the novels of M C Beaton, and the books themselves were always strapped 'A Hamish Macbeth Murder Mystery' although murders were few and far between in the TV adaptations. Music was by John Lunn.

weblinks

www.imdb.com/title/tt0111993/
www.youtube.com/watch?v=zbN2jSc5Op0
www.tv.com/hamish-macbeth/show/10189/summary.html?
en.wikipedia.org/wiki/Hamish_Macbeth_(TV_series)
www.amazon.co.uk/Hamish-MacBeth-1-3-Disc-Box/dp/B000HEZ7MK/

93. DANGER MAN

UK – ITV (Four Seasons)
Cast: Patrick McGoohan *(John Drake)*
Writer: Ralph Smart
Producers: Ralph Smart, Aida Young & Ian Stuart Black
First Broadcast (UK): 11 September 1960 – 12 January 1968
Runtime: Season 1–3 in Black & White and Season 4 in colour,
39 episodes x 25min, 45 episodes x 49min
DVD: Network 2008

Another weekend treat in 1960 was to hear the opening bars of the
Danger Man theme (by Edwin Astley, and with the theme from *The Saint*
on the flip, as a 45 rpm vinyl record fetches an eye watering fifty nicker),
and settle down to half an hour of counter espionage fun and games.
Patrick McGoohan played NATO secret service agent John Drake to the
max. There was actually little violence and womanising, unlike James
Bond for instance, as McGoohan was well against both. The series ended
in 1966, but was resuscitated in 1968 as hour-long episodes with Drake
now working for MI9, but didn't last long as McGoohan was too involved
with his next project called *The Prisoner**.

In the USA it was titled *Secret Agent Man*, and Johnny Rivers had the
hit single.

weblinks

www.imdb.com/title/tt0053496/
www.youtube.com/watch?v=2Wwm2_JJLYY
www.tv.com/danger-man/show/3620/summary.html?
www.amazon.co.uk/Danger-Man-Complete-1964-1968-Repackaged/dp/B0017LGF7I/

92. ULTRAVIOLET

UK – CH4 (One Season)
Cast: Jack Davenport (*Sgt Michael Colefield*), Susannah Harker
(*Dr Angela 'Angie' March*), Idris Elba (*Vaughan Rice*),
Philip Quast (*Father Pearse J. Harman*)
Writer: Joe Ahearne
Producer: Sophie Balhetchet
First Broadcast (UK): 15 September 1998 – 20 October 1998
Runtime: 6 episodes x 50min
DVD: E1 Entertainment 2001

Vampires are out there, and the cops are fighting them with automatic weapons loaded with carbon bullets and specialised sights that use video cameras to differentiate between vampires and humans. Plus gas grenades containing concentrated allicin, and lamps emitting ultraviolet light instead of natural sunlight, are used to kill the critters. The vampires are also science savvy, and use genetic engineering to ensure that the species continues because female vampires don't menstruate, and the males are sterile. (A bit like a few relationships I've witnessed.) They also use cars with black windows to travel by day, time locked caskets for air travel and speech synthesisers to communicate by telephone. Clever little buggers aren't they?

And no one ever uses the word 'Vampire'.

Idris Elba was one of the stars, who later went off to the USA to appear in the American version that never got shown, but it led to him auditioning for *The Wire** and the rest is history.

weblinks

www.imdb.com/title/tt0169501/
www.youtube.com/watch?v=Jwk3KeTC7HI
www.tv.com/ultraviolet/show/4940/summary.html
en.wikipedia.org/wiki/Ultraviolet_(TV_serial)
www.amazon.co.uk/Ultraviolet-Complete-Disc-Set-DVD/dp/B000053W5J/

91. FABIAN OF THE YARD

UK – BBC (Two Seasons)
Cast: Bruce Seton *(Det Superintendent Robert Fabian)*,
Robert Raglan *(Det Sgt Wyatt)*
Writer: John Davenport
Producer: John Larkin
First Broadcast (UK): 13 November 1954 – 26 March 1956
Runtime: 39 episodes x 30min in Black and White
DVD: Currently Unavailable

A real-life cop played in the old stiff upper lip way (he had to have a stiff un, as he always smoked a pipe) by Bruce Seaton. It was a big (huge) hit here, and also in the US where it was either known as *Inspector Fabian of Scotland Yard* or *Patrol Car* after the big old Humber Hawk he drove about in. An original true-life crime drama.

weblinks

www.imdb.com/title/tt0240262/
www.youtube.com/watch?v=_gT7EJvc2XQ
www.tv.com/fabian-of-the-yard/show/26611/summary.html?
en.wikipedia.org/wiki/Bruce_Seton

90. AGATHA CHRISTIE'S PARTNERS IN CRIME

UK – ITV (One Season)
Cast: Francesca Annis *(Tuppence)*, James Warwick *(Tommy)*,
Reece Dinsdale *(Albert)*
Writer: Agatha Christie
Producer: Jack Williams
First Broadcast (UK): 16 October 1983 -14 January 1984
Runtime: 10 episodes x 45min
DVD: Cinema Club 2004

Still knocking around satellite land, Tommy and Tuppence (James Warwick and a stunningly turned out Francesca Annis) play the high society detectives of the roaring twenties London where they run a three man, sorry, two man, one woman, detective agency. The third wheel is an incredibly youthful Reece Dinsdale as Albert, the movie crazy office boy, who usually gets into more trouble than a barrel-load of monkeys, and has to be rescued by the married bosses.

weblinks

www.imdb.com/title/tt0080336/
www.tv.com/agatha-christies-partners-in-crime/show/7011/summary.html
en.wikipedia.org/wiki/Agatha_Christie%27s_Partners_in_Crime
www.amazon.co.uk/Agatha-Christies-Partners-Crime-DVD/dp/

89.   COPS (US)

USA – SATELLITE (22 Seasons)
Cast: Harry Newman *(Announcer)*
Writer: John Langley
Producer: John Langley
First Broadcast (US): 11 March 1989 – Present
Runtime: 750 plus episodes x 22min
DVD: 20th Century Fox 2008

Reality TV at its most realistic, *COPS* follows police officers of every state in the union as they follow various wrongdoers down rural routes and through every major urban conurbation to the sound of *Bad Boys* by Inner Circle. There's some marvellous footage of high-speed car chases, and sometimes the poor police officers can hardly believe the stories they hear, and the excuses the perpetrators give for their misdemeanours. John Langley and Malcolm Barbour came up with the idea of *COPS* after producing several documentaries on the use of illegal drugs in the USA, during which Langley went on a drugs raid with the DEA.

Fox TV went for the pitch and the first show aired in March 1989 featuring the Broward County, Florida, sheriff's office, and still continues today with episodes popping up on all manner of satellite channels. The formula is simple: over the twenty-two minute length of each episode, three segments are included, with no narration or script. Hand held cameras bounce about, and some in-car CCTV is used. Like I said reality TV at its most realistic. All in all the show has featured 140 different cities in America, and also been filmed in Hong Kong, London and the former Soviet Union.

weblinks

www.imdb.com/title/tt0096563/
www.tv.com/cops-1989/show/28229/summary.html?
en.wikipedia.org/wiki/COPS_(TV_series)
www.amazon.co.uk/Cops-20th-Anniversary-Region-NTSC/dp/B000YDMPCE/

88. WAKING THE DEAD

UK – ITV (Eight Seasons)
Cast: Trevor Eve *(Peter Boyd)*, Sue Johnston *(Dr Grace Foley)*,
Wil Johnson *(DI Spencer Jordan)*
Writer: Barbara Machin
Producers: Colin Wratten, Barbara Machin, Susan Hogg
& Chris Ballantyne
First Broadcast (UK): 1 September 2000 – Present
Runtime: 82 episodes x 60min
DVD: 2Entertain Video 2005

Known as wanking the dead round my house, this features yet another cold case squad (aren't there enough warm ones?) in the Met, investigating the most gruesome murders outside of *Silent Witness**. Trevor Eve, another man with far too much hair for his age, is the boss, grumpy old detective Chief Inspector Peter Boyd, who is assisted by Sue Johnson as Dr Grace Foley who manages (mostly) to keep the peace.

87.   87th PRECINCT

USA (One Season)
Cast: Robert Lansing *(Det Steve Carella)*, Ron Harper *(Det Bert Kling)*
Writer: Evan Hunter
Producers: Hubbell Robinson & Winston Miller
First Broadcast (US): 25 September 1961 – 30 April 1962 in Black and White
Runtime: 30 episodes x 60min
DVD: Currently Unavailable

A genuine lost classic this one. Based on the books of Ed McBain (Evan Hunter) and filmed in stunning monochrome, *87th Precinct* cut the mustard big time. Robert Lansing played Steve Carella, top cop in the precinct.

I have almost everything that Hunter/McBain wrote, and had lunch with him once. What a nice bloke he turned out to be, unlike some writers I've revered, then met, who turned out to be arseholes. He even sent me one of his books I didn't have a few weeks later. He is sadly missed.

86.   WYCLIFFE

UK – ITV (Five Seasons)
Cast: Jack Shepherd *(Det Superintendent Charles Wycliffe)*, Helen Masters
(DI Lucy Lane), Jimmy Yuill *(DI Doug Kersey)*, Tim Wylton *(Franks)*,
Aaron Harris *(DS Andy Dixon)*, Adam Barker *(DC Ian Potter)*
Writers: Steve Trafford & Isabelle Grey
Producers: Stephen Matthews & Geraint Morris
First Broadcast (UK): 24 July 1994 – 5 July 1998
Runtime: 38 episodes x 50min
DVD: Network 2009

Why the long face Charlie? Lugubrious Jack Shepherd plays Detective
Superintendent Charles Wycliffe in these adaptations of WJ Burley's crime
novels, set in Cornwall and making good use of the scenery of the county.
But Charlie ain't a happy man. And he is even unhappier after being shot in
one episode. In fact the only time he seems pleased is when he's playing the
piano, which Shepherd does with brio.

weblinks

www.imdb.com/title/tt0108992
en.wikipedia.org/wiki/Wycliffe_(TV_series)
www.tv.com/wycliffe/show/9812/summary.html?
www.amazon.co.uk/Wycliffe-1-DVD-Jack-Shepherd/dp/B002BD9DLQ/

85.   THE STREETS OF SAN FRANCISCO

US – ITV (Five Seasons)
Cast: Karl Malden *(Det Lt Mike Stone)*,
Michael Douglas *(Inspector Steve Keller)*
Writers: Edward Hume & Carolyn Weston
Producer: Quinn Martin
First Broadcast (US): 16 September 1972 – 9 June 1977
Runtime: 120 episodes x 60min
DVD: Paramount Home Entertainment 2008

Karl Malden, the man with a nose that is beyond all comprehension, works not surprisingly the streets of San Francisco, as Det Lt Mike Stone, with his young, handsome partner Inspector Steve Keller (Michael Douglas before he became a super star). They both report to The Bureau of Inspectors Division of the police department and cover all sorts of cases. The difference is in the style of the way they approach the job. On one hand the wisdom of the older man, and on the other, the impetuosity of the younger makes for a dramatic tension that really works. Also, the location shooting does make for an exciting backdrop to the plots, as they tear around the city, and as Malden once said: 'The Streets of San Francisco has three stars: Mike Douglas, me, and San Francisco.' Pretty much like *Naked City** years before, but this time in glorious Technicolor.™

Douglas quit in 1975, and the rest of his career is history, to be replaced by Richard Hatch as Inspector Dan Robbins, but the show was never the same.

Based on a novel by Carolyn Weston, *Orphan, Poor Orphan*, which I must confess I've never read, but then Carolyn probably hasn't read any of mine, and I'm sure we're both the poorer (but hopefully not orphans) for that. Now wait a minute, another reference titles the book *Poor, Poor Ophelia*, which is probably a better title, but doesn't work for my joke, poor though that is too.

The theme was another monster, by Pat Williams, and like so many shows of the time was finished by the dramatic voiceover: 'This has been a Quinn Martin production.' Those really were the days.

weblinks

www.imdb.com/title/tt0068135/
www.youtube.com/watch?v=-F0wlfmxKdU
www.tv.com/the-streets-of-san-francisco-1972/show/1278/summary.html?
en.wikipedia.org/wiki/The_Streets_of_San_Francisco
www.amazon.co.uk/Streets-San-Francisco-Season-DVD/dp/B001CNVBLG/

84. MURDER ONE

USA – BBC2 (Two Seasons)
Cast: Mary McCormack *(Justine Appleton)*,
Michael Hayden *(Chris Docknovich)*, JC MacKenzie *(Arnold Spivak)*,
Daniel Benzali *(Ted Hoffman)*, Jason Gedrick *(Neil Avedon)*,
Antony LaPaglia *(Jimmy Wyler)*
Writers: Steven Bochco, Charles H Eglee & Channing Gibson
Producers: Steven Bochco, Charles H Eglee & Michael Fresco
First Broadcast (US): 19 September 1995 – 29 May 1997
Runtime: 41 episodes x 60min
DVD: 20th Century Fox 2005

Murder One, when it first appeared, was unique in the fact that over 23 episodes it covered only one trial. That of Neil Avedon (Jason Gedrick) a young film star accused of the murder of a teenage girl named Jessica Costello. Usually this sort of story would be covered in one episode of something like *Law and Order**, but *Murder One* followed every strand of the trial preliminaries, plus the personal lives of all concerned, especially lead defence attorney Theodore 'Teddy' Hoffman, mightily acted by the mighty figure of bald headed Daniel Benzali.

The series flopped in the US, but was reprieved for a second series, now starring Anthony LaPaglia as James Wyler. Although I'm a big fan of LaPaglia in *Without a Trace**, and even in *Frasier*, as the unlikely mockney brother of Mancunian Daphne Moon, he really doesn't cut the mustard compared with Benzali.

weblinks

www.imdb.com/title/tt0112086/
en.wikipedia.org/wiki/Murder_One_(TV_series)
www.tv.com/murder-one/show/412/summary.html?
www.amazon.co.uk/Murder-One-Season-Mary-McCormack/dp/B0002VF63S/

83. JULIET BRAVO

UK – BBC (Six Seasons)
Cast: David Ellison *(Sgt Joseph Beck)*, Noel Collins *(Sgt George Parrish)*, Stephanie Turner *(Inspector Jean Darblay)*, Anna Carteret *(Inspector Kate Longton)*, Mark Botham *(PC Danny Sparks)*, CJ Allen *(PC Brian Kelleher)*
Writer: Ian Kennedy Martin
Producers: Geraint Morris, Jonathan Alwyn & Terence Williams
First Broadcast (UK): 30 August 1980 – 31 December 1985
Runtime: 82 episodes x 50min
DVD: Cinema Club 2005

Another Saturday night favourite with a Chinese take-out, a bottle or two of wine, and possibly a spliff before bedtime, with the wife of the day.

When a female police inspector turns up to take over the station in Lancashire, in the small town of Hartley, the shit really hits the fan. The blunt northerners have no time for a lass in charge and show it. But Inspector Jean Darblay, played by Stephanie Turner, soon shows these blokes who's the boss. She's a strong woman, and with the assistance of her two sergeants, who are the first to recognise her talents, she is soon acknowledged as the queen of local crime fighting. Three years on, and Jean moves down to the soft south and another woman (Inspector Kate Longton played by Anna Carteret) takes over. 'Not more bloody women', you hear the sexist pig side of the force say. But once again girl power rules and all is well.

Created by Ian Kennedy Martin.

weblinks

www.imdb.com/title/tt0080234/
www.youtube.com/watch?v=Mpc6axb6yFl
en.wikipedia.org/wiki/Juliet_Bravo
www.tv.com/juliet-bravo/show/6783/summary.html?
www.amazon.co.uk/Juliet-Bravo-DVD-Stephanie-Turner/dp/B00090J93G/

82.   THE VICE

UK – ITV (Five Seasons)
Cast: Caroline Catz *(PC Cheryl Hutchins)*, David Harewood *(DI Joe Robinson)*, Ken Stott *(DI Pat Chappel)*
Writers: Barry Simner & Rob Pursey
Producers: Ken Baker & Rob Pursey
First Broadcast (UK): 4 January 1999 – 1 July 2003
Runtime: 28 episodes x 60min
DVD: Network 2008

Poor old Ken Stott. He has to play the most miserable sods in the world, seeing the most repugnant crimes imaginable. Remember *Messiah**? This time he's Inspector Pat Chappel of the Metropolitan Police Vice Squad around Soho and Kings Cross, and any other seedy location in London that the writers could imagine. He eats dinner standing up from takeout containers, and his sex life mainly involves prostitutes he's rescued from their pimps. Mind you, Stott has a face for it. He left after four series, and Tim Pigott-Smith, playing Detective Inspector Frank Vickers, took his place.

weblinks

www.imdb.com/title/tt0182648/
en.wikipedia.org/wiki/The_Vice_(TV_series)
www.tv.com/the-vice/show/4906/summary.html?
www.amazon.co.uk/Vice-Complete-repackaged-DVD/dp/B001JMGS68/

81. GANGSTERS

UK – BBC (Two Seasons)
Cast: Maurice Colbourne *(John Kline)*, Ahmed Khalil *(Khan)*,
Elizabeth Cassidy *(Anne Darracott)*, Alibe Parsons *(Sarah Gant)*
Writer: Philip Martin
Producer: David Rose
First Broadcast (UK): 9 September 1976 – 1 January 1978
Runtime: 12 episodes x 50min
DVD: Cinema Club 2006

Set in mid-seventies Birmingham, this multi-ethnic gangster series was vicious and violent to a fault. The first series was a big success, but the second less so. To quote from the DVD: 'On release from prison, John Kline finds the Birmingham underworld in turmoil – its leader is dead. Lawlessness spirals out of control as the White, Asian and West Indian gangs search for a new force to lead their criminality.'

And a review from the time: '*Gangsters*... brought multi-racial Britain to a mainstream audience on BBC1 as never before. Set in Birmingham's underworld, it covered, among other subjects, drug-dealing and prostitution in the nightclubs and the trading of illegal immigrants. Critics called *Gangsters* amoral, but millions of viewers – black, Asians and white – adored it.' Peter Ansorge (*The Daily Telegraph*).

Blimey, *The Telegraph* loved it. Stranger things have happened, but not many. And, the subjects covered prove that nothing much changes in thirty-five years. Worth getting the DVD set for series one, and the original *Play For Today* that kicked the whole thing off, but what followed let the whole deal down.

weblinks

www.imdb.com/title/tt0164258/
www.youtube.com/watch?v=JrTaImTusZl
www.tv.com/gangsters/show/35133/summary.html?
en.wikipedia.org/wiki/Gangsters_(TV_series)
www.amazon.co.uk/Gangsters-Complete-DVD-Maurice-Colbourne/dp/B000E1ZAAA/

80. JOHNNY STACCATO

USA – ITV (One Season)
Cast: John Cassavetes *(Johnny Staccato)*, Eduardo Ciannelli *(Waldo)*
Writer: Richard Carr
Producer: William Frye
First Broadcast (US): 10 September 1959 – 24 March 1960
Runtime: 27 episodes x 30min in Black and White
DVD: Universal Studios 2006

The wonderful John Cassavetes played Johnny Staccato, a jazz piano playing, black suit, white shirt, skinny tie wearing, part time PI, who in between entertaining the hipsters in Waldo's club in downtown NY, and chatting up glamorous women, solved cases in his downtime. Background music was supplied by the likes of Barney Kessel and Red Mitchell who played in Waldo's house band. Cassavetes himself was the poster boy for style in those days. Apart from the sharp tailoring, he smoked untipped cigarettes, and drank bourbon. There was also a hint that there was some jazz woodbines action. Reefer madness, or possibly worse. Not something a Streatham grammar school boy should aspire to, but I did, and still do. Sadly Cassavetes didn't make old bones. Elmer Bernstein's powerful theme rocketed up the charts during Christmas 1959 and still sounds the business all these years later. The following is from the liner notes of a seven inch extended play record I have of the soundtrack. I'm sure it's still copyright Capitol Records, but it was over fifty years ago, so I hope they forgive me.

'Staccato's world is one of excitement, suspense, and violence. Johnny Staccato is a private detective. He works at it because it pays well and he likes to spend money. But for sheer pleasure he's a jazz pianist – highly regarded by other musicians, but not interested in actually working as a musician. Being a young man who can devise ways to get what he wants from life, however, Staccato makes it a practice to combine his two pastimes at a place called Waldo's : a jazz hangout on MacDougal Street in Greenwich Village where he gets his calls, keeps appointments with clients, and spends his spare time playing piano with the swinging groups that work there.'

Couldn't have put it better myself, so I didn't.

79. THE ADVENTURES OF SHERLOCK HOLMES
THE RETURN OF SHERLOCK HOLMES
THE CASEBOOK OF SHERLOCK HOLMES
THE MEMOIRS OF SHERLOCK HOLMES

UK – ITV

Cast: Jeremy Brett *(Sherlock Holmes)*, David Burke *(Dr Watson)*,
Rosalie Williams *(Mrs Hudson)*

Writers: Arthur Conan Doyle & John Hawkesworth

Producer: Michael Cox

First Broadcast (UK): 24 April 1984 – 1 November 1994

Runtime: 41 episodes x 60min 5 episodes x 120min

DVD: Granada 2005

For me, there is only one Sherlock Holmes on the screen, whether it be large or small. That is Jeremy Brett. I have the complete set of 41 episodes plus 5 full-length features on 23 DVDs, which I must admit I have never watched. I'm saving them for my dotage. And if anyone says 'That'll be next week, then,' I'll cry.

Brett is exactly how I imagined Holmes to look when I started reading his adventures as a boy. Lean, haunted, white faced, with intelligence shining out of his eyes that are only sometimes dulled by drugs.

During the fifteen years that the three series and the feature length Holmes were made, two actors co-starred as Dr John Watson: David Burke in *The Adventures*, followed by the superior Edward Hardwicke in all the others.

It's all there. The locations, the costumes, the dialogue; perfect for a Sunday afternoon with tea and crumpets, or crumpet.

weblinks

www.imdb.com/title/tt0086661/
www.youtube.com/watch?v=C5AnCjSPrac
www.tv.com/sherlock-holmes-1984/show/6802/summary.html?
en.wikipedia.org/wiki/Sherlock_Holmes_(1984_TV_series)
www.amazon.co.uk/Sherlock-Holmes-Adventures-Return-DVD/dp/B0006V1FRK/

78.   BETWEEN THE LINES

UK – BBC (Three Seasons)
Cast: Neil Pearson *(Det Supt Tony Clark),*
Tom Georgeson *(Det Insp Harry Naylor),* Siobhan Redmond
(Det Sgt Maureen Connell), Tony Doyle *(Chief Supt John Deakin),*
Robin Lermitte *(Det Supt David Graves)*
Writer: J.C. Wilsher
Producer: Tony Garnett
First Broadcast (UK): 4 September 1992 – 21 December 1994
Runtime: 35 episodes x 50min
DVD: 2Entertain Video 2007

Dashing Detective Superintendent Tony Clark, (mostly dashing from one woman's bed to another, actually) played by Neil Pearson, works for the Metropolitan Police Complaints Investigation Bureau (CIB) assisted by Detective-Inspector Harry Naylor, the beautifully coiffed Tom Georgeson, and Detective Sergeant Maureen Connell played by Siobhan Redmond with a luscious mane as red as fire. In fact there's so much hair in this series I had severe Barnet envy. Tony Doyle played Chief Superintendent John Deakin who was Clark's boss, but in fact the bentest copper of them all. In the third series, for which the term 'Jumping the shark' might have been coined, the three main characters leave the force and work for a private security company actually run by Deakin. The show was executive produced by Tony Garnett, who should have called a halt to the whole thing after series two.

weblinks

www.imdb.com/title/tt0103362/
www.tv.com/between-the-lines/show/3942/summary.html?
en.wikipedia.org/wiki/Between_the_Lines_(TV_series)
www.amazon.co.uk/Between-Lines-Complete-Exclusive-Amazon-co-uk/dp

77.   77 SUNSET STRIP

USA – ITV (Six Seasons)
Cast: Efrem Zimbalist Jr *(Stuart Bailey)*, Roger Smith *(Jeff Spencer)*, Edd Byrnes *(Kookie)*
Writers: Robert C. Dennis, Montgomery Pittman, Frederick Brady, Leonard Lee & Gloria Elmore
Producers: William T. Orr & Howie Horwitz
First Broadcast (UK): 9 December 1959 – 7 February 1964
Runtime: 206 episodes x 60min in Black and White
DVD: Currently Unavailable

Along with *Johnny Staccato**, this was probably the hippest show around when I was fourteen, and Hollywood was literally just a Technicolor dream. But this was West Coast hip, much lighter than the chilliness of the East Coast. Set on the Strip itself, number 77 was situated next to Dino's, a high class restaurant where Kookie (Edd Byrnes), the coolest cat in town, parked cars and combed his hair a lot, which allowed Byrnes to have a hit record here and in the USA with *Kookie, Kookie, Lend Me Your Comb*. That wasn't the only hit from the show as an album of the soundtrack hit the charts too, but records by the main stars (Efrem Zimbalist Jr who played Stuart Bailey, and Roger Smith who played his partner Jeff Spencer) flopped.

This is how the sleeve notes from the soundtrack (probably copyright Warner Brothers Records this time) tell it: 'Music is an integral part of '*77 Sunset Strip*', and that it has contributed much to the outstanding success of the Warner Bros show is axiomatic. The light touch of comedy, interesting characters and music, which reflects the pulse of the glamorous Sunset Strip, bind the show together each week. The excitement of this fabulous boulevard of bright lights and cozy hideaways, where the good and the bad, the rich and the not-so-rich, but the always interesting, live their drama filled lives, is part and parcel of '77 Sunset Strip'.)

'Not-so-rich' you see. No poor people on that road.

weblinks

www.imdb.com/title/tt0051247/
www.youtube.com/watch?v=weAlhNDn034
www.tv.com/77-sunset-strip/show/2282/summary.html?
en.wikipedia.org/wiki/77_Sunset_Strip

76. DICK BARTON – SPECIAL AGENT

UK – ITV (Four Seasons)
Cast: Tony Vogel *(Dick Barton)*, Anthony Heaton *(Snowey White)*, James Cosmo *(Jock Anderson)*, John G. Heller *(Melganik)*
Writer: Clive Exton
Producer: Lewis Rudd
First Broadcast (UK): 6 January 1979 – 1 January 1980
Runtime: 31 episodes x 15min
DVD: Simply Media 2009

I only include this because I used to listen to it on the radio (I know, we're not doing radio, but remember the rules) at my mother's knee in the late forties. (I think. I was just a baby remember) I loved it then. The music. The cliff-hangers. Everything. This one starred Tony Vogel as Barton (never heard of him before or since), with Anthony Heaton as Snowey White and James Cosmo as Jock Anderson, two of his old army mates, always ready to lend a hand. The trio investigate the disappearance of the children of a knight of the realm, and come up against the evil Melganik (John G. Heller).

I thought he was called Mechanic, because I've met a few evil ones in my motoring history.

The show didn't catch on I'm afraid. Much like that last joke.

weblinks

www.imdb.com/title/tt0180350/
www.youtube.com/watch?v=tXugAiYcQlk
en.wikipedia.org/wiki/Dick_Barton_-_Special_Agent#Television
www.tv.com/dick-barton-special-agent/show/11407/summary.html?
www.amazon.co.uk/Dick-Barton-Special-Agent-DVD/dp/B001PQQVS8/

75.   DIAL 999

UK – ITV (One Season)
Cast: Robert Beatty *(Det Insp Mike Maguire)*
Writers: Brian Clemens, Ken Taylor, Neville Dasey,
Gil Winfield & Peter Yeldham
Producer: Harry Alan Towers
First Broadcast (UK): 8 June 1958 – 16 May 1959
Runtime: 39 episodes x 30min in Black and White
DVD: Currently Unavailable

This short-lived series always began with Robert Beatty, who starred as Mike Maguire, a Royal Canadian Mounted Policeman seconded to Scotland Yard to study advanced crime detection, (as if they'd know it if it jumped up and bit their arse, although this was fifty years ago when it was still a force) actually dialling 999 from a red call box. (I know the series was in black and white, but it must have been. They all were then.) Just think, that was in the days of press Button A to get through, or Button B to get your two pence back, (not 999 of course, that was free), the dial was round, exchanges had romantic names like CHELsea and KENsington, and if you chatted up a bird, and she deigned to give you her number, you could work out if she lived too far away to make the journey worthwhile to get a snog. NB: This was before the swinging Sixties, permissive society, the pill and peace and love, so you were actually unlikely to get more than a sweaty hand-hold on your first date.

Robert Beatty was one of many Canadian actors who stayed in post war Britain and made a fair living playing Americans in black and white B-movies.

The series was made 'with the co-operation of the Metropolitan Police and the citizens of London', though I doubt many of the citizens knew much about it, and featured much thick-eared acting by the Brits playing the baddies. Our hero, being a Mountie, always got his man. Much interest can be had from looking at the background scenes if you can actually find a copy, as it featured lots of location shots around London when the docks were still working, and the bombsites hadn't been filled in.

weblinks

www.imdb.com/title/tt0159160/
ctva.biz/UK/Dial999.htm
www.tv.com/dial-999/show/13414/summary.html?

74. CALLAN

UK – ITV (Four Seasons)
Cast: Edward Woodward *(David Callan)*, Russell Hunter *(Lonely)*,
Lisa Langdon *(Liz March)*, Anthony Valentine *(Toby Meres)*
Writer: James Mitchell
Producer: Reginald Collin
First Broadcast (UK): 8 July 1967 – 24 May 1972
Runtime: 43 episodes x 60min Black and White: (1967 – 1969)
Colour: (1970 – 1972)
DVD: Clear Vision Video 2001 & Network 2010

First appearing in the Armchair Theatre play *A Magnum For Schneider*, downbeat hitman and ex-convict David Callan, working for British Intelligence and played by Edward Woodward, was such a success that a series was commissioned. Bitter and disillusioned, Callan would try and escape from the job he hated into the world of model soldiers, which was the only place he could find peace, but he was always coerced to return by a succession of his bosses known only as Hunter (played by four actors in all, Ronald Radd, Michael Goodliffe, Derek Bond and William Squire), and the two agents who resented his place as number one man: Meres (Anthony Valentine) and Cross (Patrick Mower). Callan's only friend was Lonely, (Russell Hunter) another ex-con who'd shared a cell with Callan and whose noxious personal hygiene lent him his nickname. There was a feature film (*Callan,* 1973) which for some inexplicable reason didn't include the TV series' haunting theme, and after a final appearance in the TV play *Wet Job* (1981), Woodward went to the USA where he starred in *The Equalizer*, and as I began this book, God help us, was cameoing in *EastEnders*, which seems to be the last chance saloon for a lot of ex-cop show stars. Woodward died in 2009.

weblinks

www.imdb.com/title/tt0061238/
www.youtube.com/watch?v=IDdSWjpPJDg
www.tv.com/callan/show/3047/summary.html?
en.wikipedia.org/wiki/Callan_(TV_series)
www.amazon.co.uk/Callan-Monochrome-Years-Edward-Woodward/dp/B002ZJ1JR2/

73. Z-CARS

UK – BBC (Thirteen Seasons)
Cast: James Ellis *(Sgt Lynch),* John Slater *(Det Sgt Stone),*
Douglas Fielding *(PC Quilley),* Bernard Holley *(PC Newcombe)*
Writers: Troy Kennedy-Martin, Alan Plater & Allan Prior
Producers: Ron Craddock, David Rose & Richard Beynon
First Broadcast (UK): 2 January 1962 – 20 September 1978
Runtime: 462 episodes x 25min, 337 episodes x 50min,
Black and White: (1962 – 1970) Colour: (1970 – 1978)
DVD: Currently Unavailable

Did it really last that long? Sure it did. Z-Victor 1 and Z-Victor 2 certainly logged up some mileage as a mixed and multitudinous cast raced around

Newtown (Kirkby in Merseyside) pulling villains and birds as the cops did things that no British cops had done before. Several jobbing actors became stars in short order as the programme rocketed to the top of the charts. Stratford Johns played DCI Charlie Barlow, a detective who was not averse to dealing out rough justice of his own. He was supported by DS John Watt (Frank Windsor) who played a slightly lighter side-kick, who sometimes had to rein in his hot-headed superior.

I saw the very first one in glorious black and white (actually dark grey and light grey) on my nan's TV one Wednesday (I think) night in 1962. Bloody hell, it was water cooler moment the next day at work (actually we didn't have water coolers in 1962. The tap was good enough for us then). Now don't forget this was before the Mersey Sound and the Beatles and all that. Liverpool could have been on the other side of the world as far as we were concerned back then. Actually it still could, but that's another story. The accents were strange, the coppers were as rough as a Badger's behind, the villains were even rougher, and there was quite a lot of ultra violence. Not *Dixon of Dock Green* at all. And thank God for that. And the motors were big old Ford Zephyrs. State of the art vehicle-wise at the time.

Z-Cars soldiered on and on, despite losing Barlow and Watt to *Softly, Softly** and its successors, but it would never match those early, shocking episodes. It finally went to its happy hunting ground in 1978, but its theme tune (based on the folk song *Johnny Todd)* will always transport people of a certain age back to the Sixties.

weblinks

www.imdb.com/title/tt0129723/
www.youtube.com/watch?v=wL1HnDGTAK8
www.tv.com/z-cars/show/4039/summary.html?q=Z%20Cars&tag=search_results;summary;1
en.wikipedia.org/wiki/Z_cars

72.   THE WIRE

USA – FX, BBC2 (Five Seasons)

Cast: Dominic West *(Det James 'Jimmy' McNulty)*, John Doman
(Dep. William A. Rawls), Wendell Pierce *(Det William 'Bunk' Moreland)*,
Lance Reddick *(Lt. Cedric Daniels)*, Deirdre Lovejoy *(Rhonda Pearlman)*,
Sonja Sohn *(Det Shakima 'Kima' Greggs)*, Seth Gilliam *(Sgt Ellis Carver)*,
Domenick Lombardozzi *(Det Thomas 'Herc' Hauk)*,
Clarke Peters *(Det Lester Freamon)*

Writers: David Simon & Ed Burns

Producers: Karen L. Thorson, Nina Kostroff Noble & David Simon

Broadcast: 2 June 2002 – 9 March 2008

Runtime: 60 episodes x 60min

DVD: Warner Home Video 2008

OK. It was good, but it wasn't that good. In fact series three and four, the
school and the newspaper, were a stone drag, and even parts of the first
two could be a bore. If I wanted to look at middle-aged men wearing
headphones in a windowless room, I'd've gone to work for Radio One.

Like the fact that there are some crime writers for people who don't read
crime fiction, there are certain crime series for people who don't watch
crime shows on TV. *Guardian* readers, who over a plate of perfect risotto,
and a glass of organic Pinot Grigio, whisper conspiratorially: 'Have you
discovered *The Wire* yet?' as if it has been hidden somewhere.

Still worth watching though, if only for the gay hitman.

weblinks

www.imdb.com/title/tt0306414/
www.youtube.com/watch?v=E1ABR4UpDSU
www.tv.com/the-wire/show/8800/summary.html
www.amazon.co.uk/Wire-Complete-HBO-Season-1-5/dp/B001BBHG1S/
en.wikipedia.org/wiki/The_Wire

71. TARGET

UK – BBC (Two Seasons)
Cast: Patrick Mower *(Det Supt Steve Hackett)*, Philip Madoc *(Det Chief Supt Tate)*, Brendan Price *(Det Sgt Frank Bonney)*, Vivien Heilbron *(Det Sgt Louise Colbert)*
Writers: Bob Baker & Dave Martin
Producer: Philip Hinchcliffe
First Broadcast (UK): 9 September 1977 – 10 November 1978
Runtime: 22 episodes x 50min
DVD: Currently Unavailable

As opposition to the success of *The Sweeney** on ITV, the BBC decided to get into the act with this series, starring Patrick Mower as Detective Superintendent Steve Hackett of the Hampshire Regional Crime Squad, working mainly on the county's ports. Mower, as usual, played the sexy hardman, but for some he was too hard-nosed, and the first season was terminated early without prejudice, then in the second the violence was toned down, and there were no further episodes. Personally I preferred the first season.

weblinks

www.imdb.com/title/tt0075593/
www.tv.com/target/show/1190/summary.html
en.wikipedia.org/wiki/Target_(TV_series)

70. SILENT WITNESS

UK – BBC1 (Thirteen Seasons)
Cast: Amanda Burton *(Dr Sam Ryan)*, Tom Ward *(Dr Harry Cunningham)*, William Gaminara *(Prof. Leo Dalton)*, Emilia Fox *(Dr Nikki Alexander)*
Writers: Michael Crompton, Nigel McCrery & Tony McHale
Producers: Laura Mackie, Jessica Pope & Hilary Salmon
First Broadcast (UK): 21 February 1996 – Present
Runtime: 91 episodes x 60min, 10 episodes x 120min
DVD: 2Entertain Video 2006

Grim faced pathologist Samantha 'Sam' Ryan, played by Amanda Burton, as different a role to that of sexy Heather Huntingdon in *Brookside* as is possible to imagine. But then, you'd be grim too surrounded by all the dead bodies she had to contend with. Pus, blood, broken limbs of all shapes and sizes, bloated bodies dredged up from rivers. What a sight the BBC canteen must have been during the breaks. OK, I know most of the dead were models, but it all makes for a better story.

Before leaving the series, she was joined by Leo Dalton (William Gaminara) and Harry Cunningham (Tom Ward) who took over the reins on her departure. Latterly Emilia Fox joined the team as Nikki Alexander.

weblinks

www.imdb.com/title/tt0115355/
www.youtube.com/watch?v=IRUS9dSHLjQ
www.bbc.co.uk/programmes/b007y6k8
en.wikipedia.org/wiki/Silent_Witness
www.tv.com/silent-witness/show/3983/summary.html
www.amazon.co.uk/Silent-Witness-Complete-BBC-DVD/dp/B000F3T8YQ/

69. ROCKFORD FILES

US – BBC (Six Seasons)
Cast: James Garner *(Jim Rockford)*, Noah Beery Jr *(Joseph 'Rocky' Rockford)*, Joe Santos *(Dennis Becker)*
Writers: Stephen J. Cannell & Roy Higgins
Producers: Stephen J. Cannell, Meta Rosenberg, Charles Floyd Johnson & David Chase
First Broadcast (US): 13 September 1974 – 10 January 1980
Runtime: 123 episodes x 60min
DVD: Universal 2005

Always beginning with the voice of James Garner who played Jim Rockford (presumably so he didn't get confused when being called to makeup) on his answering machine, Rockford was a down at heel ex-con, wrongfully jailed for five years in San Quentin for a robbery he didn't commit, (blimey, I think we've been here before) who, upon his release, decided to help out others in the same predicament. Assisted by his father, (Joseph 'Rocky' Rockford played by Noah Beery Junior) Jim hated violence and rarely carried a gun or for that matter got paid for the cases he solved. And we've been there many times too.

weblinks

www.imdb.com/title/tt0071042/
vodpod.com/watch/55836-rockford-files-season-1-intro
www.tv.com/the-rockford-files-1974/show/1276/summary.html
en.wikipedia.org/wiki/The_Rockford_Files
www.amazon.co.uk/Rockford-Files-1-DVD/dp/B000AV3QXC/

68. NO HIDING PLACE

UK – ITV (Ten Seasons)
Cast: Raymond Francis *(Chief Det Supt Tom Lockhart)*,
Eric Lander *(Det Insp Harry Baxter)*, Johnny Briggs *(Det Sgt Russell)*,
Michael McStay *(Det Sgt Perryman)*
Writer: Bill Strutton
Producers: Ray Dicks & Peter Wiles
First Broadcast (UK): 16 September 1959 – 22 June 1967
Runtime: 236 episodes x 60min in Black and White
DVD: Currently Unavailable

From Cliff's first hit to the summer of love, *No Hiding Place* really did rack up 235 episodes over eight years. Detective Chief Superintendent Lockhart, once again played by Raymond Francis, previously the lead in *Murder Bag** and *Crime Sheet*, this time partnered by Detective Sergeant Baxter (Eric Lander) who proved so popular he went off to star in Echo Four Two, and was replaced by Johnny Briggs who went on to be Mike Baldwin in *Coronation Street*. When the series was cancelled in 1965, the public demanded it be reinstated which it was.

weblinks

www.imdb.com/title/tt0159898/
www.youtube.com/watch?v=dV28B1_HAEs
www.tv.com/no-hiding-place/show/12548/summary.html
en.wikipedia.org/wiki/No_Hiding_Place

67. MIDNIGHT CALLER

USA – BBC1 (Three Seasons)

Cast: Gary Cole *(Jack 'Nighthawk' Killian)*, Dennis Dun *(Billy Po)*,
Arthur Taxier *(Lt. Carl Zymak)*, Wendy Kilbourne *(Devon King)*

Writer: Richard Di Lello

Producers: Robert Singer & Jim Michaels

First Broadcast (US): 25 October 1988 – 17 May 1991

Runtime: 61 episodes x 60min

DVD: Currently Unavailable

Jack 'Nighthawk' Killian, played by Gary Cole, is king of the night time
airwaves on San Francisco's KJCM (98.3 FM) radio station. An ex-cop who
killed his own partner by accident, riddled with guilt (unlike his partner who
was riddled with bullets. One bullet actually, but who cares?). He quit the
force and struck lucky with a new showbiz career. Jack takes phone calls
from all sorts of dodgy characters who have the troubles of the world on
their shoulders. He solves crimes, aids the unfortunate and generally makes
a nuisance of himself to the real cops including his old buddy Lt Carl Zymak
(Arthur Taxier).

This used to be shown late on in the listings, as it deserved, but sadly this is
the kind of series you'd never find on BBC1 these days.

weblinks

www.imdb.com/title/tt0094510/
www.tv.com/midnight-caller/show/2610/summary.html
en.wikipedia.org/wiki/Midnight_Caller

66. LOVEJOY

UK – BBC (Six Seasons)
Cast: Ian McShane *(Lovejoy)*, Dudley Sutton *(Tinker Dill)*,
Chris Jury *(Eric Catchpole)*, Phyllis Logan *(Lady Jane Felsham)*
Writers: Terry Hodgkinson, Ian La Frenais, Roger Marshall
& Jonathan Gash
Producers: Allan McKeown & Tony Charles
Broadcast: 10 January 1986 – 4 December 1994
Runtime: 71 episodes x 50min
DVD: Delta Home Entertainment 2004

The saviour of many a long, winter's afternoon on Gold channel, Lovejoy plied his trade in the boondocks of East Anglia as a dodgy antiques expert/ salesman/valuer/forger. Played beautifully by Ian McShane, Lovejoy ducked and dived up and down the M11 in a Morris Traveller, assisted by Tinker and Eric (Dudley Sutton and Chris Jury) and pursued the lovely Lady Jane Felsham (Phyllis Logan) whenever her husband was away. (And sometimes when he wasn't.) The one thing that always amazed me was that Lovejoy could get from Norwich or close, to London, conduct his dodgy business, and back home, all in one summer's afternoon. I can tell you I've been stuck on that road for hours.

Adapted from the novels of Jonathan Gash.

weblinks

www.imdb.com/title/tt0090477/
www.youtube.com/watch?v=aylTQSZYeiA
en.wikipedia.org/wiki/Lovejoy
www.tv.com/lovejoy/show/1511/summary.html
www.amazon.co.uk/Lovejoy-Complete-Collection-DVD/dp/B000ALVT8G/

65. HAWAII FIVE-O

US – ITV (Twelve Seasons)
Cast: Jack Lord *(Det Steve McGarrett)*, James MacArthur *(Danny)*,
Kam Fong *(Chin Ho)*, Herman Wedemeyer *(Duke)*, Zulu *(Kono Kalakaua)*
Writer: Leonard Freeman
Producers: James Heinz & Leonard Freeman
First Broadcast (US): 20 September 1968 – 4 April 1980
Runtime: 272 episodes x 60min
DVD: Paramount 2009

Two things make *Hawaii Five-O* one of the greats. The theme by Morton Stevens over the opening titles (I've got a great version by *The Ventures*), and the catchphrase 'Book 'em Danno – Murder One,' which always wound up a successful investigation. Two things, plus Jack Lord as the immaculately suited, cool as ice detective Steve McGarrett who leads the Five-O team, assisted by Danny Williams as the previously mentioned Danno.

Beautiful locations, great seventies boats of cars, and lots of running around, kept the show in the ratings for over ten years.

A new series of *Hawaii 5-0* has just started showing in the States with Alex O'Loughlin as Steve McGarrett. This apparently is not a remake but a 'reimagining' of the original series.

weblinks

www.youtube.com/watch?v=AepyGm9Me6w
www.imdb.com/video/cbs/vi3287484185/
www.imdb.com/title/tt0062568/
www.imdb.com/media/rm2453312000/tt0062568?slideshow=1
en.wikipedia.org/wiki/Hawaii_Five-O
www.mjq.net/fiveo/
www.youtube.com/watch?v=rLKdYXyQa90
www.tv.com/hawaii-five-o-1968/show/1277/episode.html
www.amazon.co.uk/Hawaii-Five-O-First-Season-DVD/dp/B000JU7M02/

64. EDGE OF DARKNESS

UK – BBC (One Season)
Cast: Bob Peck *(Ronald Craven)*, Joe Don Baker *(Darius Jedburgh)*, Charles Kay *(Pendleton)*, Ian McNeice *(Harcourt)*, Joanne Whalley *(Emma Craven)*
Writer: Troy Kennedy Martin
Producer: Michael Wearing
First Broadcast (UK): 4 November 1985 – 9 December 1985
Runtime: 6 episodes x 50min
DVD: 2Entertain Video 2003

One of the classics of the genre that literally changed the way crime fiction was presented on TV. So popular was it on its inaugural run on BBC2 that it was immediately repeated on BBC1. From Eric Clapton's doomy theme as a train full of nuclear waste rumbles thorough the dark to its finale, which I won't reveal lest you have never seen it, but will now, it rocked my world.

weblinks

www.imdb.com/title/tt0090424/
www.tv.com/edge-of-darkness/show/14004/summary.html
en.wikipedia.org/wiki/Edge_of_Darkness
www.amazon.co.uk/Edge-Darkness-Complete-bob-peck/dp/B00004CYR0/

63. BERGERAC

UK – BBC (Nine Seasons)
Cast: John Nettles *(Det Sgt Jim Bergerac)*, Terence Alexander *(Charlie Hungerford)*, Sean Arnold *(Chief Insp Barney Crozier)*
Writer: Robert Banks Stewart
Producers: Jonathan Alwyn & Robert Banks Stewart
First Broadcast (UK): 18 October 1981 – 26 December 1991
Runtime: 6 episodes x 90min, 87 episodes x 50min
DVD: 2Entertain Video 2009

When sexy Trevor Eve quit *Shoestring**, leaving a load of spare scripts, the producers cleverly relocated them to Jersey, and brought in John Nettles, another housewife's choice, and retitled the series *Bergerac*. Initially only intended as a stopgap, the show took off big style and lasted ten years. Bergerac is yet another alcoholic, maverick, off the reservation policeman, who drives an unusual car (a 1941 Triumph TR1 Sports this time), keeps going back to the bottle, chases women all over the island, and even has a bit of a fling with a suspected jewel thief (Liza Goddard), and has a far too intimate (not that kind) relationship with his ex-father-in-law Charlie Hungerford (Terence Alexander) who is as crooked as a corkscrew. But once again true love conquers all and Bergerac falls for beautiful Frenchwoman Danielle Aubry (Thérèse Liotard) and moves to Provence to become a private detective, which for some reason entailed many visits to Jersey to work on cases. But by this time the show had, as they say, 'Jumped the shark.'

weblinks

www.imdb.com/title/tt0081831/
en.wikipedia.org/wiki/Bergerac_(TV_series)
www.tv.com/bergerac/show/2392/summary.html
www.amazon.co.uk/Bergerac-Complete-Collection-John-Nettles/dp/B002KSA41A/
www.youtube.com/watch?v=U8hsj_CqrOs

62. LIFE ON MARS

UK – BBC (Two Seasons)
Cast: John Simm *(Sam Tyler)*, Philip Glenister *(Gene Hunt)*,
Liz White *(Anne Cartwright)*, Dean Andrews *(Ray Carling)*,
Marshall Lancaster *(Chris Skelton)*
Writers: Matthew Graham, Tony Jordan & Ashley Pharoah
Producers: Jane Featherstone, Matthew Graham,
Claire Parker & Marcus Wilson
First Broadcast (UK): 9 January 2006 – 10 April 2007
Runtime: 16 Episodes x 60min
DVD: Contender Entertainment Group 2007

One day in 2006, DCI Sam Tyler (John Simm) is walking down a Manchester street, listening to David Bowie on his iPod, when he's hit by a car. When he comes to, he's in 1973, and the same song (*Life on Mars*, natch) is blasting out of the 8-track (ah, such fond memories of the one I had in an orange Capri, and how small the back seat was) in his Rover. Confused, he heads for the local cop shop to find he's been transferred there, and he's now a DI, who's introduced to his new boss DCI Gene Hunt, played to the hilt by Philip Glenister. (The strange thing is that Hunt/Glenister is now an icon of non political correctness, as the UK becomes more and more PC, Health & Safety obsessed, and, quite frankly, heading down a road that can only end in a cul-de-sac of lost freedom.)

Glenister plays Hunt like he's just stepped out of an episode of *The Sweeney**, and poor old Sam has to change his style whilst still wondering what happened to the 21st Century, as well as being bombarded by strange dreams and a TV that talks back to him. Also, there's the shape of the appealing WPC Annie Cartwright (Liz White) who he has more than a passing interest in, plus he even meets his mother and his four-year-old self.

A second series tried, quite unsuccessfully I'm afraid, to tie up all the loose ends, and Sam ended up committing suicide. Or did he? We'll never know, as Simm got tired of the series and left.

Unfortunately the BBC couldn't let a good thing die with Sam, and thus appeared the awful *Ashes to Ashes* with the dreadful Keeley Hawes as Alex Drake, a female cop also transported back in time (the 80s now). I lasted ten minutes of the first episode and turned over to something on Channel 5.

weblinks

www.imdb.com/title/tt0478942/
www.tv.com/life-on-mars-uk/show/51334/summary.html
en.wikipedia.org/wiki/Life_on_Mars_(TV_series)
www.amazon.co.uk/Life-Mars-Complete-BBC-Disc/dp/B000LPQDBO/

61. RUMPOLE OF THE BAILEY

UK – ITV (Seven Seasons)
Cast: Leo McKern *(Horace Rumpole)*, Jonathan Coy *(Henry)*,
Julian Curry *(Claude Erskine-Brown)*, Marion Mathie *(Hilda Rumpole)*
Writer: John Mortimer
Producers: Jacqueline Davis & Lloyd Shirley
First Broadcast (UK): 3 April 1978 – 1 December 1992
Runtime: 42 episodes x 60min
DVD: Freemantle Home Entertainment 2008

Rumpole of the Bailey, a cop show? Surely not. Listen bud, if I say it is, it is. And anyway, who puts Horace Rumpole's defendants in the dock? Cops of course.

Played like the trouper he was, Leo McKern takes John Mortimer's character and makes him his own. Based in Lincoln's Inn, he is often merely tolerated by the other barristers in the practice, but does bring home the bacon, mainly from a family of South London villains who constantly need his expertise. At home in 38 Froxbury Mansions, Kensington he is in constant fear of his wife, Hilda (She Who Must Be Obeyed played by a pair of gimlet eyed actresses, Peggy Thorpe Bates and Marion Mathie, but not at the same time, obviously) although, in fact, they have a loving relationship, especially when the red wine is uncorked and his cigar lit to his satisfaction. Otherwise he is happiest in Pomeroy's wine bar enjoying a bottle of Chateau Fleet Street. God knows what he'd make of the smoking ban these days. In fact dear Horace would probably detest England in the 21st Century, not without cause.

In fact Rumpole all started on BBC1 as a one off, in the *Play for Today* series on BBC1 in 1975. Auntie didn't see a future in the character (silly them) and Mortimer took his character to the opposition, where he happily stayed for years.

weblinks

www.imdb.com/title/tt0078680/
en.wikipedia.org/wiki/Rumpole_of_the_Bailey
www.tv.com/rumpole-of-the-bailey/show/2123/summary.html
www.amazon.co.uk/Rumpole-Bailey-1-7-Complete-DVD/dp/B001G55AJE/

60. MISS MARPLE

UK – BBC1 (Twelve feature length episodes)
Cast: Joan Hickson *(Miss Marple)*, David Horovitch *(Chief Inspector Slack)*,
Ian Brimble *(Det Sergeant Lake)*
Writers: Agatha Christie & TR Bowen
Producers: George Gallaccio & Guy Slater
First Broadcast (UK): 26 December 1984 – 27 December 1992
Runtime: (DVD) 16 x 50min, 1 x 114min, 3 x 110min, 1 x 100min
DVD: 2Entertain Video 2005

There have only ever been two Miss Marples for me. On the big screen it was
Margaret Rutherford, but as we're talking TV here, it has to be Joan Hickson
who wins the red balloon. Broadcast intermittently between 1984 and 1992,
the shows appear to have been made in an earlier, simpler time, with a
patina that perfectly fits the post-war world in which they are all set, despite
when the original stories were written. Similar to *Midsomer Murders**, the
beauty of the locations (Nether Wallop mostly) is set against the viciousness
of the murders and of the villains that Jane Marple susses out, much to the
chagrin of David Horovitch as a perpetually frustrated Chief Inspector Slack.
The period is perfectly illustrated as young men in sports cars romancing
pretty girls in floaty summer dresses. The butchers, bakers and grocers all
seem to have plenty of goods in stock despite rationing, and the sun shines
beautifully down over the blood-soaked countryside.

Agatha Christie's Marple, switched to ITV, starring firstly Geraldine McEwan
and, latterly, Julia Mackenzie, like the remake of *Minder** is best avoided.

weblinks

www.imdb.com/title/tt0088833/
www.youtube.com/watch?v=fmQIxN3NA4U
www.tv.com/miss-marple/show/61787/summary.html
en.wikipedia.org/wiki/Miss_Marple_(TV_series)
www.amazon.co.uk/Agatha-Christie-Miss-Marple-Collection/dp/B0007ZD6W2/

59. MARK SABER

USA – ITV

Cast: Tom Conway & Donald Gray *(Inspector Mark Saber),*
James Burke *(Det Sgt Tim Maloney)*

Writers: Wallace Bosco, William Wolff and others

Producers: Guy V. Thayer Junior & Roland D. Reed

First Broadcast (UK): 'MARK SABER' 20 June 1957 – 6 February 1959

Runtime: B&W 65 episodes x 30min

First Broadcast (UK): 'SABER OF LONDON' 16 November 1959 – 30 April 1962

Runtime: 91 episodes x 30 min (the actual number is unclear)

DVD: Currently Unavailable

Initially played by Tom Conway in the USA, Mark Saber soon washed up on Blighty's shores in the shape of Donald Gray as the one-armed detective. Wouldn't it have been interesting if he'd appeared in *The Fugitive** where a one-armed man did it? Maybe not on second thoughts. Saber was another suave devil, beautifully dressed and equally at home in London slums and the flesh pots of Europe. In *Mark Saber* he was assisted by Stephanie Ames (Diane Decker) and Barney O'Keefe (Michael Balfour).

Later on, Gray returned as *Saber of London* (No messing about with this bloke. He owns the town) and used his false arm to bash up villains of every stripe. Later on Gray voiced Colonel White in *Captain Scarlet and the Mysterons*.

weblinks

www.imdb.com/title/tt0043215/
en.wikipedia.org/wiki/Donald_Gray
www.78rpm.co.uk/tvs.htm
www.memorabletv.com/showss/saberoflondon.htm
www.whirligig-tv.co.uk/tv/adults/other/marksaber.htm

58. FIVE DAYS

UK – BBC
Cast: Hugh Bonneville *(DSI Iain Barclay)*, Janet McTeer
(Det Sergeant Amy Foster), David Oyelowo *(Matt Wellings)*,
Edward Woodward *(Vic Marsham)*
Writer: Gwyneth Hughes
Producers: Hilary Salmon & Caroline Skinner
First Broadcast (UK): 23 January 2007 – 1 February 2007
Runtime: 5 episodes x 60min
DVD: Metrodome 2007

A young mother vanishes from the side of the road whilst going to buy a bunch of flowers for her father, who she is visiting with her two children. When mum doesn't return, the youngsters do a runner, so there's now three people to find. The five hours of the show each covers one day in the search and eventual explanation of exactly what happened, and who was responsible. Hugh Bonneville played Detective Superintendent Iain Barclay, and Janet McTeer appeared as his fierce and loyal sidekick, Detective Sergeant Amy Foster.

A second series of *Five Days* was shown on BBC One in March 2010, but it bore no resemblance to this one.

weblinks

www.imdb.com/title/tt0840094/
www.tv.com/five-days/show/67852/summary.html
en.wikipedia.org/wiki/Five_Days
www.bbc.co.uk/programmes/b006t6lm
www.amazon.co.uk/Five-Days-Complete-BBC-Disc/dp/B000PMGRJQ/

57. THE AVENGERS / THE NEW AVENGERS

UK – ITV (Seven Seasons)
Cast: Patrick Macnee *(John Steed)*, Diana Rigg *(Emma Peel)*,
Honor Blackman *(Catherine Gale)*, Ian Hendry *(Dr David Keel)*,
Linda Thorson *(Tara King)*
Writers: Brian Clemens, Philip Levene & Roger Marshall
Producers: Brian Clemens, Albert Fennell & Julian Wintle
First Broadcast (UK): 7 January 1961 – 21 May 1969
Runtime: 161 episodes x 50min with some in Black and White
DVD: Optimum Home Entertainment 2009

I can still remember sitting in on one Saturday night way back in 1961, and watching the first edition of *The Avengers*. And believe me, it was a very different bird from what it became as the Sixties began to swing, and the series went all rainbow. (No, not the one with Bungle the Bear. Colour, I mean). In those early days, *The Avengers* was a very dark series. A spin-off from a show called *Police Surgeon*, which I vaguely remember from my school days. It starred Ian Hendry as Dr David Keel who, after his girlfriend is murdered by a drugs gang, enlists the help of an MI5 agent named John Steed (Patrick Macnee) to help avenge (geddit?) her death. The story runs for several episodes, then Hendry leaves and Steed teams up with the short lived Dr Martin King (Jon Rollason) and nightclub singer Venus Smith (Julie Stevens) before the arrival of the first real Avengers tough woman character, Cathy Gale (Honor Blackman).

At this juncture, the series moved up a gear, as Blackman comes across like some Soho dominatrix, tricked out in skin tight leather and kicking arse all over the shop. Steed himself settles for eccentric Savile Row suits, drives a Bentley, sports a bowler and rolled umbrella which he often uses as a weapon, and lives in some luxury in Kensington or Knightsbridge. (Macnee and Blackman also made a bid for pop stardom singing *Kinky Boots* in 1964. Quite a collector's item now on original 7 inch single. A mint copy will set you back thirty-five quid.)

Honor Blackman quit the show to play Pussy Galore in *Goldfinger* later that year, so enter Diana Rigg as Mrs Peel. This is when the show really took off, went to colour and became the by-word for swinging London, Carnaby Street, King's Road et al.

The Yanks loved the show, which featured a sort of merrie olde England with picture postcard villages and all sorts of London locations. Cleverly, the producers nearly always filmed in deserted streets, with only the main characters in shot, making the shows eerie to view.

When Rigg left, Linda Thorson joined the cast as Tara King, but the writing was on the wall.

In the mid-seventies, the *New Avengers* arrived with Macnee reprising his role as Steed, joined by the annoying Joanna Lumley as Purdey and the equally annoying Gareth Hunt, the king of coffee ads, as Mike Gambit. Forget it.

The original theme was written by Johnny Dankworth, but the one that everyone remembers was by Laurie Johnson.

weblinks

www.imdb.com/title/tt0054518/
en.wikipedia.org/wiki/The_Avengers_(TV_series)
www.tv.com/the-avengers/show/1196/summary.html
www.amazon.co.uk/Avengers-Surviving-Episodes-DVD/dp/B002GPNKFO/

56. WHITECHAPEL

UK – BBC (One Season)
Cast: Rupert Penry-Jones *(DI Joe Chandler)*, Philip Davis *(DS Ray Miles)*, Alex Jennings *(Commander Anderson)*, Johnny Harris *(DC Sanders)*, Steve Pemberton *(Edward Buchan)*, Sam Stockman *(DC Kent)*, George Rossi *(DC McCormack)*
Writers: Ben Court & Caroline Ip
Producers: Julie Clark, Sally Woodward Gentle & Marcus Wilson
First Broadcast (UK): 2 February 2009 – 18 February 2009 ,
11 October – 25 October 2010
Runtime: 3 episodes x 60min, 3 episodes x 60min
DVD: 2Entertain Video 2009

In 2008, strange things start happening in Whitechapel, East London. Strange and horrifying things that mirror the murders committed by Jack the Ripper one hundred and twenty years earlier.

The case pricks the interest of the media, and Commander Anderson of the Metropolitan Police (Alex Jennings) calls in a young, ambitious, and most of all media savvy Detective Inspector just waiting for more promotion on the fast track. DI Joseph Chandler is played by Rupert Penry-Jones, late of Spooks*, as a rather posh individual a bit out of his depth in the close-knit murder team led by Detective Sergeant Ray Miles, played by Phil Davis, who resent the introduction of a policeman they see as only interested in his own career. In fact Chandler is as determined to catch the murderer as they are.

Eventually, as we knew they must, the team meld together and catch the Ripper.

Another series was mooted to be filmed. Then I read that, because of budget cuts, it was cancelled. Then again I heard it had been recommisioned again. In fact it now has and had the team chasing a reconstituted Kray twins.

weblinks

www.imdb.com/title/tt1186356/
www.tv.com/five-days/show/67852/summary.html
en.wikipedia.org/wiki/Whitechapel_(TV_series)
www.amazon.co.uk/Whitechapel-DVD-Rupert-Penry-Jones/dp/B001MDI9I4/

55. 55 DEGREES NORTH

UK – BBC (Two Seasons)
Cast: Don Gilet *(Nicky)*, Christian Rodska *(Dennis)*, Jaeden Burke *(Matty)*, George Harris *(Uncle Errol)*, Dervla Kirwan *(Claire)*, Mark Stobbart *(Martin)*, Andrew Dunn *(Sgt Rick Astel)*
Writer: Timothy Prager
Producers: Adrian Bate, Barbara McKissack & Timothy Prager
First Broadcast (UK): 6 July 2004 – 10 July 2005

Runtime: 14 episodes x 60min
DVD: 2Entertain Video 2006

Don Gilet starred as DS Dominic 'Nicky' Cole, an honest copper who blew the whistle on a crooked colleague in the Met and was transferred to Newcastle (hence the title, which refers to the geographical difference from London to the city) where he's met with contempt and relegated to the position of night detective (actually named *The Night Detective* in the USA). A quirky little series featuring a strong ethnic cast, with some comedy capers, but serious issues also, as Gilet (currently pretty well wasted in *EastEnders* as a mental psychopath/preacher) tries to overcome the prejudice he faces as a black whistleblower, and win the respect of the suspicious Northern coppers he's forced to work with, and at the same time resuscitate his police career.

Inevitably, there's a tough boss, DI Dennis Carter (Christian Rodska) who starts off detesting the man, but eventually recognises Nicky's talent for police work, and inevitably there's a racist uniformed copper (Sgt Rick Astel – Andrew Dunn) who also inevitably ends up as a friend. And inevitably again there's a tasty female prosecutor (Dervla Kirwan) who takes more than a shine to the night detective.

Then there's a domestic angle as Nicky lives with his Uncle Erroll (George Harris) and his nephew Matty (Jaeden Burke) in a nice cottage by the sea, inevitably with a nosy widowed neighbour who takes a shine to Uncle Erroll. But Nicky should be careful as salt air would play havoc with the paint work of the vintage white Mercedes that somehow he manages to afford to run.

It's a shame it ended so soon.

weblinks

www.imdb.com/title/tt0397756/
www.bbc.co.uk/drama/55degrees/
www.tv.com/55-degrees-north/show/24642/summary.html
en.wikipedia.org/wiki/55_Degrees_North
www.amazon.co.uk/55-Degrees-North-Don-Gilet/dp/B000F9RAE0/

54. THE SHIELD

USA – CH5 (Seven Seasons)

Cast: Michael Chiklis *(Detective Vic Mackey)*,
Catherine Dent *(Officer Danny Sofer)*, Walton Goggins
(Detective Shane Vendrell), Michael Jace *(Officer Julien Lowe)*,
Jay Karnes *(Detective Holland Wagenbach)*, Benito Martinez
(Captain David Aceveda), CCH Pounder *(Detective Claudette Wyms)*,
Kenneth Johnson *(Detective Curtis 'Lemonhead' Lemansky)*
Writer: Shawn Ryan
Producer: Shawn Ryan
First Broadcast (US): 12 March 2002 – 25 November 2008
Runtime: 89 episodes x 60min
DVD: Sony Pictures Home Entertainment 2009

Feeling safe in your beds tonight? If you lived in East Los Angeles you'd feel a lot safer if Detective Vic Mackey (Ross Kemp lookalike Michael Chiklis) and his buddies from the elite Strike Team, based at a run down station known as The Barn, were policing the area. That is, unless you're a gangbanging drug dealer, then Vic et al might come visiting. Possibly to arrest you. Possibly to shoot you down in cold blood, but definitely to relieve you of some or all of your ill-gotten gains, and any narcotics you might carelessly leave lying around.

The rest of the team are Detective Shane Vendrell (Walton Goggins), Detective Curtis 'Lemonhead' Lemansky (Kenneth Johnson), overseen by Captain David Aceveda (Benito Martinez).

weblinks

www.imdb.com/title/tt0286486/
en.wikipedia.org/wiki/The_Shield_ (TV_series)
www.tv.com/the-shield/show/8261/summary.html
www.amazon.co.uk/Shield-1-7-DVD-Michael-Chiklis/dp/B001UL7SMG/

53. MISSION: IMPOSSIBLE

USA – ITV (Seven Seasons)
Cast: Greg Morris *(Barney Collier)*, Peter Lupus *(Willy Armitage)*,
Bob Johnson *(Person on Tape)*, Peter Graves *(James Phelps)*
Writer: Bruce Geller
Producer: Bruce Geller
First Broadcast (US): 17 September 1966 – 30 March 1973
Runtime: 171 episodes x 50 min
DVD: Paramount 2006

My mission, which I chose to accept, is to write about one of the tastiest crime series of them all. The IMF (Impossible Mission Force obviously) are a disparate bunch of individuals, all experts in their particular fields, and all dedicated to making the world a safe place for Americans. The boss of the IMF, firstly Daniel Briggs (Steven Hill), then latterly, the late Peter Graves as Jim Phelps, picks up his instructions by tape recorder in a phone booth, or by parcel post that self destructs after five seconds, together with a bundle of photographs of his target(s). He then sorts through the photos of his own team and chooses who is to work on any particular task. The force consisted of Rollin Hand (Martin Landau), master of disguise, Muscle man Willie Armitage to handle the heavy work (Peter Lupus), Sexy Cinnamon Carter (Barbara Bain, wife of Landau and every man's fantasy. Mine anyway), Barney Collier (Greg Morris. A breakthrough part for a black actor at the time) electronics expert. When Landau quit, Leonard Nimoy joined the team as Paris. Yeah, just Paris, but with normal ears.

The action generally took place in South America or Eastern Europe as the IMF thwart the plans of swarthy gentlemen in fancy uniforms. The series was reconstructed in the late eighties and filmed in Australia, still with Graves, but the tape was replaced by a disc. The location was changed because of a writers' strike in Hollywood, and then there were several big screen outings starring Tom Cruise, which really didn't work. (My Chevrolet truck was in the first one.) Lalo Schifrin wrote the theme, one of the most memorable, and best, ever. And he never, ever did not choose to accept the mission.

52. PIE IN THE SKY

UK – BBC (Five Seasons)

Cast: Richard Griffiths *(Henry Crabbe)*, Maggie Steed *(Margaret Crabbe)*, Malcolm Sinclair *(ACC Freddy Fisher)*

Writers: Andrew Payne, John Milne & Richard Maher

Producers: Chrissy Skinns, Allan McKeown & Joanna Willett

First Broadcast (UK): 13 March 1994 – 17 August 1997

Runtime: 40 episodes x 60 min

DVD: Acorn Media 2006

Another series that was never going to be contentious, as cuddly Detective Inspector Henry Crabbe (possibly too cuddly, as surely no copper would be allowed to be that seriously obese and keep his job) played by Richard Griffiths who literally fills the screen, together with his accountant wife Margaret (Maggie Steed) as well as crime busting runs a superior restaurant, Pie In The Sky of the title, in the town of Middleton (actually Hemel Hempstead) which is always close to fiscal disaster because of Henry's decision to always use the finest and most expensive ingredients, and also employ a bunch of idiots to work for him. Classic stuff though, closer to *Hetty Wainthropp Investigates** than *The Shield**.

Don't knock it, there's room for both, and sometimes it's good to settle down with a glass of wine and a bag of Mini Doritos (sorry Henry, I know you'd hate them) and not have to think too hard.

51. MERSEY BEAT

UK – BBC (Four Seasons)
Cast: Michelle Holmes *(Sgt Connie Harper)*,
Haydn Gwynne *(Supt Susan Blake)*
Writers: Nick Saltrese, Joe Ainsworth & Chris Murray
Producers: Mal Young & Chris Murray
First Broadcast (UK): 16 July 2001 – 19 January 2004
Runtime: 38 episodes x 60 min
DVD: Currently Unavailable

Pretty much what you'd imagine from the title, though maybe not if you're of a certain age, and a fan of *The Beatles* and *Gerry and the Pacemakers*. So, sadly not a jolly romp through the history of The Cavern Club, but instead a cop series set in Liverpool, although the first three series are actually located in Runcorn, Cheshire, only the final one being relocated to the city itself. In fact, it's more of a soap really, concentrating mainly on the personal lives and troubles of the cops. There's a strong female presence as well, as the bosses of the station are largely women.

Although I thoroughly enjoyed it, it was a critical and popular failure, though it still managed to stagger through four series, which I doubt would happen these days. In the third series, to try and put up the ratings, they introduced sexy Leslie Ash (before the unfortunate cosmetic surgery) as Inspector Charlie Eden and Mark Womack as DI Peter Hammond, (he must be quite used to playing Liverpool cops, as he also appeared in *Liverpool One*), but to no avail, and the series sank. (Sank, Mersey, geddit?)

weblinks

www.imdb.com/title/tt0289817/
en.wikipedia.org/wiki/Merseybeat_(TV_series)
www.tv.com/merseybeat/show/7369/summary.html

50. A MAN CALLED IRONSIDE

USA – BBC1 (Eight Seasons)
Cast: Raymond Burr *(Robert T. Ironside)*, Don Galloway
(Det Sgt Ed Brown), Don Mitchell *(Mark Sanger)*
Writer: Collier Young
Producer: Cy Chermak
First Broadcast (US): 28 March 1967 – 16 January 1975
Runtime: 197 episodes x 60 min & 3 x 120 min
DVD: Anchor Bay 2008

Chief of San Francisco Detectives Robert T. Ironside, played by Raymond Burr, is crippled by an assassin's bullet in the first episode of this long running series. Committed to a wheelchair he convinces the powers that be that he may be allowed to continue as a detective, or at least a consultant to those more mobile police officers. He converts an attic inside police headquarters into a work/living space and a police van into a mobile office. He is minded by Mark Sanger (Don Mitchell) an ex-gang banger who cares for his day to day needs, and is assisted by Detective Ed Brown (Don Galloway) and ex beauty queen Barbara Anderson as Officer Eve Whitfield, who later quit the show and moved to *Mission: Impossible*, and was replaced by Elizabeth Baur as policewoman Fran Belding.

Burr was no stranger to hit TV shows as he played Perry Mason for nine years previous to making the TV movie that sired *Ironside*, as it was known in the US. Burr's grumpy persona was perfect for the frustrated man of action, and he ruled the airwaves on both sides of the Atlantic. The memorable theme was composed by Oliver Nelson.

weblinks

www.imdb.com/title/tt0061266/
www.youtube.com/watch?v=zNS0u6USBT8
www.tv.com/ironside/show/974/summary.html
en.wikipedia.org/wiki/Ironside_(TV_series)
www.amazon.co.uk/Ironside-1-DVD-Raymond-Burr/dp/B0013URJUA/

49. THE FUGITIVE

USA – ITV (Four Seasons)
Cast: David Janssen *(Dr Richard Kimble)*, William Conrad *(Narrator)*,
Barry Morse *(Lt. Philip Gerard)*
Writer: Roy Huggins
Producers: Quinn Martin & Alan A. Armer
Broadcast (UK): 17 September 1963 – 29 August 1967
Runtime: 120 episodes x 60 min
Black and White: Seasons 1 – 3 Colour: Season 4
DVD: Paramount Home Entertainment 2008

Wrongly imprisoned for a crime he did not commit (not again surely?) Doctor David Kimble (David Janssen) escapes from a prison train and goes on the trail of the one-armed man he saw running from his house where his wife lay dead. Pursued all the time by Lieutenant Philip Gerard (Barry Morse) Kimble drifts from town to town, working poorly paid jobs, but managing to stay clean and tidy and pull dozens of beautiful women on the way. Of course he had to abandon them at the end of the episode, and carry on his quest, until eventually in a two-part episode, so eagerly anticipated by fans of the show, that, like *Lost** this year, it was shown at the same time all over the world.

Now that's fame.

weblinks

www.imdb.com/title/tt0056757/
en.wikipedia.org/wiki/The_Fugitive_(TV_series)
www.tv.com/the-fugitive-1963/show/312/summary.html
www.youtube.com/watch?v=DBXb_6-2zOw
www.amazon.co.uk/Fugitive-Season-Complete-Volumes-DVD/dp/B0010BTMAC/

48. CRACKER

UK – ITV (Four Seasons)

Cast: Robbie Coltrane *(Dr Eddie 'Fitz' Fitzgerald)*,

Geraldine Somerville *(DS Jane 'Panhandle' Penhaligon)*,

Kieran O'Brien *(Mark Fitzgerald)*, Barbara Flynn *(Judith Fitzgerald)*

Writer: Jimmy McGovern

Producer: Sally Head

First Broadcast (UK): 27 September 1993 – 27 November 1995

Runtime: 23 episodes x 60 min 1 episode x 100 min 1 episode x 120 min

DVD: ITV Studios Home Entertainment 2008

Edward 'Fitz' Fitzgerald is a larger than life character in more ways than one. A boozer, smoker, gambler, overweight womaniser, he's perfectly played by Robbie Coltrane. Fitz is a criminal psychologist working for the Manchester police. The series was a huge success with Coltrane winning a BAFTA. It ran for three series, but sadly came back for a two-hour special set in Hong Kong which was a mistake, but allowed the cast and crew to get kitted out in cheap silk suits. Or so I heard.

There was a disastrous US remake called *Fitz*, starring Robert Pastorelli, in 1998 but I doubt you'd find it, even on the most remote satellite channel.

weblinks

www.imdb.com/title/tt0105977/
en.wikipedia.org/wiki/Cracker_(UK_TV_series)
www.youtube.com/watch?v=npe_vZ1TkIM
www.tv.com/cracker/show/9851/summary.html
www.amazon.co.uk/Cracker-Complete-Collection-Robbie-Coltrane/dp/B001CWLFI6/

47. SOFTLY, SOFTLY
SOFTLY SOFTLY-TASK FORCE

UK – BBC (Twelve Seasons)
Cast: Stratford Johns *(Charlie Barlow)*, Frank Windsor *(John Watt)*
Writers: Alan Plater, Elwyn Jones & Gerry Davis
Producer: Leonard Lewis
First Broadcast (UK): 5 January 1966 – 15 December 1976
Runtime: 264 episodes x 60min Black and White: Seasons 1 – 5
Colour: Seasons 6 – 12
DVD: Currently Unavailable

After leaving *Z-Cars** the double act of Detective Superintendent Charlie Barlow (Stratford Johns) and Detective Chief Inspector (later Detective Chief Superintendent) John Watt (Frank Windsor) teamed up again in *Softly, Softly* and *Softly, Softly – Task Force*, as they headed down the highway from Merseyside to the soft southern city of Wyvern (actually Bristol) where they meet their old mate Sergeant Blackitt, now retired, also relocated south, and running a newsagent's shop. Plus some new colleagues, the most important being Inky the police dog and his handler Police Constable Henry Snow (Terence Rigby), and Inspector Harry Hawkins (Norman Bowler) who gave the show some sex appeal. Inky did too, but only to bitches.

I still remember the shock when Inky was killed, and carried away by Henry Snow in floods of tears.

Later, in *Barlow At Large*, the pair moved to London. And finally Johns starred in the eponymous *Barlow*. Blimey, the bloke had nine lives. In the death, Barlow and Watt teamed up once more in a forgettable series called *Second Verdict*, which frankly I can't remember at all.

weblinks

www.imdb.com/title/tt0129717/
en.wikipedia.org/wiki/Softly,_Softly_(TV_series)
www.tv.com/softly-softly/show/8544/summary.html

46.   THE PROFESSIONALS

UK – ITV (Five Seasons)
Cast: Gordon Jackson *(George Cowley),*
Martin Shaw *(Doyle),* Lewis Collins *(Bodie)*
Writer: Brian Clemens
Producers: Brian Clemens, Albert Fennell & Raymond Menmuir
First Broadcast (UK): 30 December 1977 – 6 February 1983
Runtime: 57 episodes x 60 min
DVD: E1 Entertainment 2006

Oh what fun they had, Bodie and Doyle, running, jumping, standing still, driving souped-up Ford Escorts and Capris, shooting guns and snogging birds, whilst their boss the dour George Cowley scowled in the background. The two heroes (Lewis Collins and Martin Shaw, nicknamed Golliwog if I dare use that word because of his extravagant curly barnet) are members of Criminal Intelligence Five, bossed by Gordon Jackson's Cowley.

Much spoofed and having a bad rep, the repeats in the afternoon on satellite actually reveal it to be a pretty decent action adventure series, although the cars are in fact a bit pathetic compared with their American counterparts, and a terrible theme that sort of ripped off *Shaft*.

weblinks

www.imdb.com/title/tt0075561/
www.imdb.com/media/rm3227423744/tt0075561?slideshow=1
www.youtube.com/watch?v=GH7VFJjDhVU
www.tv.com/the-professionals/show/3191/summary.html
www.personal.u-net.com/~carnfort/Professionals/
en.wikipedia.org/wiki/The_Professionals_(TV_series)
www.amazon.co.uk/Professionals-Vol-1-DVD/dp/B0009YVBKK/

45. MAIGRET

UK – ITV (Two Seasons)
Cast: Michael Gambon *(Chief Inspector Jules Maigret)*,
Geoffrey Hutchings *(Sgt Lucas)*, Jack Galloway *(Inspector Janvier)*,
James Larkin *(Inspector LaPointe)*
Writer: Georges Simenon
Producers: Sally Head & Arthur Weingarten
First Broadcast (UK): 11 February 1992 – 18 April 1993
Runtime: 12 episodes x 60 min
DVD: Network 2007

Some purists may cry that the sixties series of *Maigret*, starring Rupert
Davies with the haunting theme by Ron Grainer, was the perceived version,
but the Parisian detective appeared on the screen played by several actors,
including Richard Harris, and this series starring Michael Gambon as Maigret
and Geoffrey Hutchings as his faithful sidekick Lucas is my favourite. Filmed
in Budapest because of its resemblance to the Paris of the time when the
novels by George Simenon were set, and it's cheaper.

weblinks

www.imdb.com/title/tt0107221/
www.tv.com/maigret-1992/show/27461/summary.html
en.wikipedia.org/wiki/Maigret_(1992_TV_series)
www.youtube.com/watch?v=TT9VvFSoCgE
www.amazon.co.uk/Maigret-1-2-Complete-DVD/dp/B000RJEIT8/

44. HIGHWAY PATROL

USA – ITV (Four Seasons)
Cast: Broderick Crawford *(Dan Mathews)*,
William Boyett *(Sgt Ken Williams)*, Art Gilmore *(Narrator)*
Writers: Jack Rock, Don Brinkley, Bob Mitchell,
Hendrik Vollaerts & Lou Huston

Producer: Frederick W. Ziv
First Broadcast (US): 3 October 1955 – 1 September 1959
Runtime: 156 episodes x 30 min in Black and White
DVD: Currently Unavailable

It took a big man to head the highway patrol of a sprawling, unnamed western state and bring the bad guys to justice every week for five years, and Broderick Crawford was perfect for the job. He drove the interstates and back roads in his big V8 engined squad car, and faced down criminals of every stripe with just a 'Ten-four' (message received and understood), 'Ten-twenty' (report your position), and 'Put out an APB' (All Points Bulletin) on the radio, and a pistol in his hand. There were car chases and gunfights aplenty, and oh how I wanted to be a highway patrolman. Great theme tune too.

weblinks

www.imdb.com/title/tt0047739/
www.youtube.com/watch?v=yxcep0eJR-8
www.tv.com/highway-patrol/show/1036/summary.html?q=highway%20
patrol&tag=search_results;summary;1
www.highwaypatroltv.com/photos.shtml
en.wikipedia.org/wiki/Highway_Patrol_(TV_series)
www.amazon.com/Highway-Patrol-Show-DVD-Complete/dp/B000B89A8O/

43. THE CLOSER

USA – CHANNEL 4 (Six Seasons)
Cast: Kyra Sedgwick *(Deputy Chief Brenda Leigh Johnson)*, JK Simmons *(Assistant Chief Will Pope)*, Corey Reynolds *(Sgt David Gabriel)*, Robert Gossett *(Commander Taylor)*, GW Bailey *(Detective Lt. Provenza)*, Jon Tenney *(Agent Fritz Howard)*
Writer: James Duff
Producers: James Duff, Gil Garcetti, Greer Shephard & Michael M.Robin
First Broadcast (US): 27 September 2005 – Present
Runtime: 75 episodes x 60 min
DVD: Warner Home Video 2007

With a corn pone accent you could cut with a knife, mush-mouthed Kyra Sedgewick playing Deputy Chief Brenda Leigh Johnson transfers from Atlanta, Georgia to Los Angeles to run the Priority Homicide Division of the LAPD, much to the chagrin of many of the macho male detectives, but soon proves that her ability to close cases (hence the title) makes her the perfect person for the job. And by Christ, she's horny too. Imagine that voice whispering sweet nothings in the dark.

weblinks

www.imdb.com/title/tt0458253/
www.tv.com/the-closer/show/28972/summary.html
en.wikipedia.org/wiki/The_Closer
www.amazon.co.uk/Closer-1-Complete-DVD/dp/B000K0YPII/

42. ADAM ADAMANT LIVES!

UK – BBC (Two Seasons)
Cast: Gerald Harper *(Adam Adamant)*, Juliet Harmer *(Georgina Jones)*,
Jack May *(William E. Simms)*
 Writer: Dick Vosburgh
Producer: Verity Lambert
First Broadcast (UK): 3 June 1966 – 25 March 1967
Runtime: 29 episodes x 50 min in Black and White
DVD: 2Entertain Video 2006

Something like Sherlock Holmes, but a bit more of an action man, Adam Llewellyn De Vere Adamant (Gerald Harper) is a crime buster in Victorian England. When he comes a cropper to his nemesis, known only as 'The Face', a leather masked nasty piece of work, he is injected with a preservative drug and encased in a block of ice. Fast forward to London at its swingingest in 1966 and, still frozen somehow, Adam is discovered by a bunch of workmen and thawed out. Of course that would be right, I don't think.

Bit of a culture shock I'd say, but the confused man is rescued by the dolliest of dolly birds, Georgina Jones (Juliet Harmer. Whatever happened to her?)

who actually knows of his exploits all those years ago via her old granddad, and saves his bacon.

Now complete with a manservant (Jack May), a former music hall artist, Adamant and Georgina (driving a Mini Cooper S) set out to clean the capital of criminals once more in a sort of *Avengers** vibe, still dressed like a geezer from the turn of the century, and toting a sword as his main weapon of choice. Brilliant stuff and some episodes were directed by Ridley Scott. Say no more.

Theme sung by Kathy Kirby.

weblinks

www.imdb.com/title/tt0059963/
www.youtube.com/watch?v=V96-kvbZwQk
en.wikipedia.org/wiki/Adam_Adamant_Lives
www.tv.com/adam-adamant-lives!/show/8909/summary.html
www.amazon.co.uk/Adam-Adamant-Lives-Complete-Collection/dp/B0006GVKB6/

41. THE FIXER

UK – ITV (Two Seasons)
Cast: Andrew Buchan *(John Mercer)*, Jody Latham *(Calum McKenzie)*, Tamzin Outhwaite *(Rose Chamberlain)*, Peter Mullan *(Lenny Douglas)*
Writers: Ben Richards & Neil Cross
Producers: Jane Featherstone, Christopher Hall, Faith Penhale & Ben Richards
First Broadcast (UK): 3 March 2008 – 6 October 2009
Runtime: 12 episodes x 60 min
DVD: 2Entertain Video 2008

John Mercer (Andrew Buchan) is in jail for a murder when, suddenly, he's on the out. But his freedom is short lived when he's coerced by Lenny Douglas (Peter Mullan) into working for his unofficial, and decidedly dodgy, off the reservation operation, targeting criminals other cops can't touch for one reason or another. Mercer's brief – kill 'em, and let God sort them out.

Living in the Goldfinger-designed block of flats on the north side of the Blackwall tunnel is a young villain named Calum (Jody Latham). A doper, thief, music and woman crazy, young layabout, he's also under Lenny's thumb, and Mercer moves into his flat, much to his disgust at the ramshackle state of it. The only bright spot is Rose (Tamzin Outhwaite) who sleeps with Mercer once, then withholds her favours, also much to his chagrin. Mercer kicks against his orders to kill, but Douglas constantly has the upper hand.

The second series moves the gang to the North Peckham estate (or maybe the Aylesbury), but doesn't work as well. Maybe it's because Buchan is also appearing in some dreadful costume drama on the other side as a defence attorney. And, sadly, the wig he wears doesn't suit.

weblinks

www.imdb.com/title/tt1204507/
www.youtube.com/watch?v=h4lEQGxlLcw&feature=related
en.wikipedia.org/wiki/The_Fixer_(TV_series)
www.tv.com/the-fixer/show/75455/summary.html
www.amazon.co.uk/Fixer-1-DVD-Tamzin-Outhwaite/dp/B0015083NK/

40. HETTY WAINTHROPP INVESTIGATES

UK – BBC1 (Four Seasons)
Cast: Patricia Routledge *(Hetty Wainthropp)*, Dominic Monaghan *(Geoffrey Shawcross)*, Derek Benfield *(Robert Wainthropp)*, John Graham-Davies *(DCI Adams)*
Writers: John Bowen & David Cook
Producers: Laura Mackie & Jo Wright
First Broadcast (UK): 3 January 1996 – 4 September 1998
Runtime: 27 episodes x 60 min
DVD: Acorn Media 2008

Heavens above! Another soft centred show. I must be getting old. You see, I bow to no one for my admiration of Patricia Routledge who plays the Lancashire pensioner turned private eye. From the doleful theme tune to the miserable streets that she rides with her assistant Geoffrey Shawcross

(Dominic Monaghan, the smack head rock star in *Lost**, and what a change of image that was), firstly on the back of his scooter, and later in a sickly yellow Volkswagen Beetle convertible supplied by his new girlfriend, Janet (Suzanne Maddock aka WPC Cass Rickman in *The Bill**. Lumme, as they'd say in *Dick Barton – Special Agent**, these actors do get about). Hetty Wainthropp, like the Mounties, always gets her man (or woman). The cases are mundane in the main, but Routledge does what she always does, puts in a workmanlike (workwomanlike?) appearance, and brings a likeable aspect to what could have been a snoopy old dragon of a character. Like *Miss Marple** before her, she constantly bemuses the local police force in the shape of John Graham Davies as DCI Adams, who eventually actually calls on her for help. The series was devised by David Cook, from his novel *Missing Persons*.

weblinks

www.imdb.com/title/tt0127376/
www.tv.com/hetty-wainthropp-investigates/show/3955/summary.html
en.wikipedia.org/wiki/Hetty_Wainthropp_Investigates
www.youtube.com/watch?v=NiV94u2gYvg
www.amazon.co.uk/Hetty-Wainthropp-Investigates-Collection-Complete/dp/

39. CRIMINAL MINDS

US (Five Seasons)
Cast: Shemar Moore *(Derek Morgan),* Matthew Gray Gubler
(Dr Spencer Reid), Thomas Gibson *(Aaron 'Hotch' Hotchner),*
AJ Cook *(Jennifer 'JJ' Jareau),* Kirsten Vangsness *(Penelope Garcia),*
Mandy Patinkin *(Jason Gideon)*
Writer: Jeff Davis
Producers: Gigi Coello-Bannon, Erica Messer,
Deborah Spera & Simon Mirren
First Broadcast (US): 22 September 2005 – Present
Runtime: 114 episodes x 45 min
DVD: Walt Disney Studios 2007

Special agent Jason Gideon, played by Mandy Patinkin, leads the FBI's elite profiling team, who specialise in analysing the most evil men and women in America. Second in command is Aaron Hotchner (Thomas Gibson). The rest of the team are Elle Greenway, an expert on sexual offences, Derek Morgan (Shemar Moore) who pinpoints obsessional crimes, Dr Spencer Reid (Matthew Gray Gubler) a genius but damaged, and Jennifer 'JJ' Jareau (A.J. Cook) the rookie of the squad. The team is on constant alert and ready to fly anywhere in the USA at a moment's notice.

Catchphrase: 'Wheels up in twenty minutes.'

weblinks

www.imdb.com/title/tt0452046/
en.wikipedia.org/wiki/Criminal_minds
www.tv.com/criminal-minds/show/33484/summary.html
www.cbs.com/primetime/criminal_minds/
www.amazon.co.uk/Criminal-Minds-Season-Complete-DVD/dp/B000M2E7G4/

38. COLD CASE

USA – SKY (Seven Seasons)
Cast: Kathryn Morris *(Lilly Rush),* John Finn *(John Stillman),*
Jeremy Ratchford *(Nick Vera),* Thom Barry *(Will Jeffries)*
Writer: Meredith Stiehm
Producers: Jerry Bruckheimer & Jonathan Littman
First Broadcast (US): 28 September 2003 – 2 May 2010
Runtime: 156 episodes x 60 min
DVD: Currently Unavailable

Cold Case follows a formula, and a successful one, as it has now had six series, and more to come (I hope). Always starting with a flashback to the time and scene of a particular crime, shot in the cinema, or later, television style of the day; black and white for the forties or early fifties, psychedelic for the sixties and so on. Then fast-forward to present day Philadelphia where the cold case squad operate and either new evidence is found, or a witness or family member comes forward with information or seeking closure. Then the cops go into the vaults where all evidence is stored in boxes. Mind you, knowing some of the cops I've met, I'm surprised the paperwork etc. is so easy to find. After that, they start to delve into the past until the crime is solved. And finally, the victim is shown to watch the cop who cracks it, before slowly vanishing. The show stars the weirdly attractive Kathryn Morris as Detective Lily Rush, who has the look of an alien left behind by her spaceship.

Music is most important to the show, depicting the era of the crime, and due to licensing problems the series has never appeared on DVD.

Shame.

weblinks

www.imdb.com/title/tt0368479/
www.youtube.com/watch?v=ugfzs5KR7pg&feature=related
www.tv.com/cold-case/show/16989/summary.html
en.wikipedia.org/wiki/Cold_Case_(TV_series)
www2.warnerbros.com/television/tvShows/coldcase/

37.   A TOUCH OF FROST

UK – ITV (Fifteen Seasons)
Cast: David Jason *(DI Frost)*, Bruce Alexander *(Supt Mullett)*, John Lyons *(D.S. Toolan)*
Writer: RD Wingfield
Producers: Richard Bates, Philip Burley & David Reynolds
First Broadcast (UK): 6 December 1992 – 5 April 2010
Runtime: 34 episodes x 100 min 6 episodes x 75 min
DVD: Playback 2004

I was first introduced to Detective Inspector Jack Frost by a friend of mine (now sadly deceased, but not forgotten) when, after a weekend of debauchery at her cottage in Suffolk, she gave me RD Wingfield's first novel, also entitled *A Touch Of Frost*. To tell you the truth, I didn't fancy it from the jacket, and plot synopsis. But in those days I had to beg or borrow books, so eventually I started it, and loved it. Got the rest up until Wingfield died a while back. Then along came the TV adaptation starring David Jason, and I think I've seen every single one. Some, several times I admit.

Set in fictional Denton (now I always suspected Denton was based in Guildford where I lived for a while. To paraphrase the late, great Johnny Cash: 'Guildford, you was a living hell to me'. The only good thing coming out of it being the A3 heading towards London. The old ones are the best! In fact some of it was shot in Leeds. Go figure.) Jack Frost was the archetypal, grumpy maverick, old school copper who would not come into the warmth of the new way of policing, much to the chagrin of his boss Superintendent Mullett, beautifully played by Bruce Alexander. Frost didn't do paperwork. Frost didn't do filing. Frost didn't do computers. Frost didn't do touching his forelock to the great and good. Frost also didn't do salads, living mostly on a diet of the full English, bacon sarnies, take-out curry and Chinese. So how does he survive in the new, cuddly police service? I hear you ask. Well Jack has one ace up his sleeve. He won the George Cross for heroism, and the Chief Constable loves him. Also, he's a bloody good cop.

Jason shines as Frost, but he's no spring chicken, and eventually, at age seventy or thereabouts, in a job where the retirement age is the mid-fifties, it all had to end, and earlier this year, so it did. But how? Me, I'd've loved to see Frost go out in a hail of bullets, but no. Apparently there were three endings shot, and of course the wimps at ITV went for the soft option. Enter Phyllis Logan as an RSPCA inspector who gets Jack involved in a dog fighting case, and they fall in love. Do pass the sick bag someone. Phyllis is no spring chicken for sure, but Jason is really looking his age. The show faded out forever as they go off into the sunset in a local park, looking from the front like a considerate daughter taking her elderly father for a constitutional, and from behind like a zookeeper taking a chimpanzee for an outing.

RIP Frost.

weblinks

www.imdb.com/title/tt0108967/
en.wikipedia.org/wiki/A_Touch_of_Frost_(TV_series)
www.itv.com/frost/
www.tv.com/a-touch-of-frost/show/3804/summary.html
www.amazon.co.uk/Touch-Frost-1-5-DVD/dp/B0002VF4I0/

36. SHOESTRING

UK – BBC1 (Two Seasons)
Cast: Trevor Eve *(Eddie Shoestring)*, Michael Medwin *(Don Satchley)*,
Liz Crowther *(Sonia)*, Doran Godwin *(Erica Bayliss)*
Writers: Robert Bennett, Robert Banks Stewart & Richard Harris
Producer: Robert Banks Stewart
First Broadcast (UK): 30 September 1979 – 21 December 1980
Runtime: 21 episodes x 50 min
DVD: BBC

Trevor Eve played Eddie Shoestring as another loser. This time an ex-computer wizard, boozer, who had a nervous breakdown and ended up in a mental facility, decided to become a private detective who, in the first episode, did an investigation as a favour for Don Satchley (Michael Medwin) the boss of Radio West in an easily recognisable Bristol. Shoestring is subsequently hired by the station on the recommendation of Sonia, the gloriously buxom, bespectacled, redheaded Liz Crowther, daughter of Leslie, to run investigations for listeners when all other methods have failed. Shoestring was occasionally helped in his investigations by his on/off girlfriend who also acted as his landlady, the extremely annoying Erica Bayliss (Doran Godwin) who played an unlikely barrister so she could obtain information for Eddie when he was stumped, which was often.

Eve, catnip to the ladies I believe, was soon racking up massive viewer figures, but decided to knock the character on the head and go back to his first love – live theatre, which led creator Robert Banks Stewart, with a bunch of redundant scripts on his hands, to relocate the location to Jersey to invent *Bergerac** as another alcoholic, rehab bound car crash waiting to happen, starring another housewife's choice, John Nettles, and the rest is history.

weblinks

www.imdb.com/title/tt0078690/
www.youtube.com/watch?v=nX_rMu2K7as
www.tv.com/shoestring/show/5599/summary.html
en.wikipedia.org/wiki/Shoestring_(TV_series)
www.amazon.co.uk/Shoestring-episodes-Private-Find-lady/dp/B000VC0KAM/

35. SPECIAL BRANCH

UK – ITV (Four Seasons)
Cast: Derren Nesbitt *(Det Chief Insp Jordan)*, George Sewell *(Det Chief Insp Alan Craven)*, Morris Perry *(Charles Moxon)*, Fulton Mackay *(Det Chief Supt Inman)*, Roger Rowland *(Det Sgt Bill North)*, Keith Washington *(Det Con. Morrissey)*, Patrick Mower *(Chief Insp Tom Haggarty)*
Writers: George Markstein, Roy Bottomley & Tom Brennand
Producers: Lloyd Shirley & George Taylor
First Broadcast (UK): 17 September 1969 – 9 May 1974
Runtime: 53 episodes x 60 min
DVD:Network 2008

The first two series of *Special Branch* were made by Thames Television and shot on videotape, and boy does it show. Those two, beginning in 1969, starred Derren Nesbitt as Detective Inspector Jordan, and the wonderfully named Wensley Pithey as Superintendent Eden, and Fulton Mackay as Detective Superintendent Inman. Latterly, Euston Films arrived and the series moved, not surprisingly, to film, and starred Detective Chief Inspector Alan Craven (George Sewell) and Detective Chief Inspector Tom Haggarty (Patrick Mower), looking like he'd just stepped off the bus from the King's Road after spending a small fortune in the trendiest boutique in the place. Sewell and Mower chased around London in fast cars, sporting shooters, as they worked undercover (or covers in Mower's case, as he certainly had an eye for the ladies, and vice versa) foiling all manner of villains looking to ruin the Queen's peace.

weblinks

www.imdb.com/title/tt0063953/
www.youtube.com/watch?v=_Y9aLvoJyfE&feature=fvw
en.wikipedia.org/wiki/Special_Branch_(TV_series)
www.tv.com/special-branch/show/3044/summary.html
www.amazon.co.uk/Special-Branch-1-4-Complete-DVD/dp/B001B8CBM0/

34. RESNICK: LONELY HEARTS & ROUGH TREATMENT

UK – BBC1 (Two Seasons)
Cast: Tom Wilkinson *(Det Insp Charlie Resnick)*
Writers: John Harvey
Producers: Colin Rogers
First Broadcast (UK): 31 March 1992 – 25 July 1993
Runtime: 5 episodes x 50 min
DVD: Currently Unavailable

Based on the novels by John Harvey, Charlie Resnick is another maverick copper, this time of Polish origin and based in Nottingham, living alone but for a load of pussies (not that sort) and living mostly on strong coffee, strong booze and sandwiches from his favourite deli, often eaten standing up over the sink, listening to his massive jazz collection. Ah, the romance of it all.

Resnick, played by Tom Wilkinson, didn't last long on network TV as it was as downbeat as was possible without actually slowing to a standstill. I loved the show but, like so many of its ilk, it vanished without trace. Actually that's not totally true as I think Resnick has appeared on radio since, but then we're not talking radio here.

weblinks

www.imdb.com/title/tt0251371/
www.imdb.com/title/tt0105238/
en.wikipedia.org/wiki/Charlie_Resnick

33. PRIME SUSPECT

UK – ITV (Seven Seasons)
Cast: Helen Mirren *(DCI Jane Tennison)*, Tom Bell *(DS Bill Otley)*,
John Benfield *(DCS Michael Kernan)*, John Bowe *(George Marlow)*,
Zoe Wanamaker *(Moyra Henson)*
Writer: Lynda La Plante

Producers: Sally Head & Don Leaver
First Broadcast (UK): 7 April 1991 – 22 October 2006
Runtime: 3 episodes x 101–105 min 11 episodes x 200 – 207 min
DVD: ITV Studios Home Entertainment 2008

Feminist copper Jane Tennison, played by Helen Mirren, initially a Detective Chief Inspector, latterly Detective Superintendent, takes over the case of a prostitute brutally murdered in grungy old London town when the senior detective keels over with a fatal heart attack. So we're shown that the only way for a woman to succeed in the Metropolitan Police is to fill dead men's shoes. Naturally she solves the case, but only by becoming a sort of surrogate bloke, smoking, boozing and shagging. *Prime Suspects Two* to *Five* duly followed, as Tennison moved around from London to Manchester, ingesting vodka by the bottleful as she went, and keeping tobacco companies in business. Linda La Plante then went on to make *The Red Dahlia* with Kelly Reilly playing a sort of Tennison junior, with possibly the most annoying voice and fringe in showbiz. Avoid like the plague.

weblinks

www.imdb.com/title/tt0098898/
www.youtube.com/watch?v=8Xs122nMt7A
en.wikipedia.org/wiki/Prime_Suspect
www.tv.com/prime-suspect-uk/show/3927/summary.html
www.amazon.co.uk/Prime-Suspect-Complete-Collection-DVD/dp/B001CWLFDG/

32. KOJAK

US – BBC (Five Seasons)
Cast: Telly Savalas *(Lt. Theo Kojak)*, Dan Frazer *(Capt. Frank McNeil)*, Kevin Dobson *(Det Bobby Crocker)*, George Savalas *(Det Stavros)*
Writers: Abby Mann & Selwyn Raab
Producers: James Duff McAdams & Matthew Rapf
First Broadcast (US): 24 October 1973 – 18 March 1978
Runtime: 2 episodes x 120 min 1 episode x 180 min

115 episodes x 60 min

DVD: ITV Studios Home Entertainment 2008

Who loves ya baby? Just about everyone at the time of only three channels, when Kojak emptied the pubs for an hour or so on a Saturday night. Lt Theodore 'Theo' Kojak of the NYPD, played to the hilt by bald-headed Telly Savalas in designer gear that featured Concorde sized lapels, big flares and ties that could blind a horse. Kojak bent the rules, but always came through for the folks of the Manhattan South 13th precinct. This show spawned all sorts of spin-offs and merchandise. A Corgi Toys model of his brown (all cars were brown at the time for some reason. I even had a brown 1600 Ford Cortina Ghia automatic. Wow! That's living alright) Buick, lollipops sporting his visage, and even a dreadful No 1 single of David Gates' song 'If' which was more spoken than sung in the style of Lee Marvin's I Was Born Under A Wandering Star. Neither record features heavily in the collector's market, I might add.

The supporting cast in the show was exceptional. Kevin Dobson played Kojak's young partner, Lieutenant Bobby Crocker. Dan Frazer played Chief McNeil, and George Savalas (Yes, his brother, but with a full head of hair. I wonder if Telly was jealous. Telly, jelly?) as Stavros.

But all was not well in Kojakland, and in 1993, a year before he died, Savalas sued Universal TV for six million dollars he claimed in unpaid royalties.

There was a remake in 2005 starring the wonderfully named, but soon forgotten, except by his mum I imagine, Ving Rhames. Don't even think about it.

weblinks

www.imdb.com/title/tt0069599/
www.youtube.com/watch?v=EExXoKg5xdU
en.wikipedia.org/wiki/Kojak
www.tv.com/kojak/show/143/summary.html
www.amazon.co.uk/Kojak-1-DVD-Telly-Savalas/dp/B0009NS9HY/

31. MESSIAH

UK – BBC1 (Five Seasons)
Cast: Ken Stott *(DCI Red Metcalfe,)* Frances Grey *(Kate Beauchamp),*
Neil Dudgeon *(DI Duncan Warren),* Art Malik *(DCS Sam Emerson),*
Sam Troughton *(Thomas Stone),* Helen McCrory *(Dr Rachel Price),*
Beatie Edney *(Grace Eccleshall)*
Writers: Lizzie Mickery, Terry Cafolla & Boris Starling
Producers: Robert Cooper, Louise Berridge, Kate Triggs,
James M. Dowaliby & Charlie Woodhouse
First Broadcast (UK): 26 May 2001 – 21 January 2008
Runtime: 9 episodes x 90 min
DVD: 2Entertain Video 2004, BBC

Based on a novel by Boris Starling, *Messiah* is the first case for DCI Red
Metcalfe, played by Ken Stott. Goodness gracious, but life is no fun for our
Ken is it? In the first series, during a heat wave, dead bodies are found with
their tongues cut out and a silver spoon inserted. Could this be anti-public
school boy revenge? No. It's all down to religion and the Bible.

In *Messiah 2* (the programmes actually feature Roman numerals to make
them more spooky) things get no better for Ken. This time his brother is
found knifed to death in Leadenhall Market. Another day, another serial
killer, but this time it's personal (yawn).

Messiah 3 shows shortcomings in the NHS as a murderer stalks a hospital.
And then, as you might have guessed, up popped *Messiah 4*.

The series were a success, but a lot of viewers balked at the blood and gore,
which once upon a time would have been banned as a video nasty, and took
the horror about as far as prime time BBC TV would allow.

weblinks

www.imdb.com/title/tt0249301/
www.tv.com/messiah/show/62299/summary.html
en.wikipedia.org/wiki/Messiah_(TV_series)
www.amazon.co.uk/Messiah-Complete-BBC-Ken-Stott/dp/B0002IAQVI/

30. DRAGNET

USA – ITV (Eight Seasons)
Cast: Jack Webb *(Sgt Joe Friday)*, George Fenneman
(Announcer Opening), Hal Gibney *(Announcer Closing)*
Writers: Jack Webb, James E. Moser & John Robinson
Producers: Michael Meshekoff, Stanley D. Meyer & Jack Webb
First Broadcast (US): 16 December 1951 – 23 August 1968
Runtime: 276 episodes x 30 min in Black and White
DVD: Elstree Hill Entertainment 2008

Catchphrases galore in this early American cop show. In fact the first to be screened here in 1955, on Channel Nine as it was known then: 'Ladies and gentlemen, the story you are about to see is true. Only the names have been changed to protect the innocent.'

That was the opening voiceover, coupled with the amazing theme by Walter Schumann, which has hit the charts three times in its history (way back in the time of 78 rpms by Ray Anthony and Ted Heath, and then again in 1987 by Art Of Noise), and introduced Jack Webb as LAPD Detective Sergeant Joe Friday, 'Just the facts Ma'am: I carry a badge. That's my job.'

The show went on for years, later as *Badge 714* (Friday's number) then *Dragnet 68, 69* and *70*. After Webb's death it was revived again, and there was even a spoof movie starring Dan Akroyd and Tom Hanks, which more or less pissed on the good memories of the show. But not mine.

weblinks

www.imdb.com/title/tt0043194/
www.imdb.com/media/rm1820301312/tt0043194?slideshow=1
www.tv.com/dragnet-1951/show/20239/summary.html
en.wikipedia.org/wiki/Dragnet_(series)
www.amazon.co.uk/Dragnet-TV-8-DVD-Set/dp/B0011UY6F8/

29. HARRY O

USA – BBC (Two Seasons)

Cast: David Janssen *(Harry Orwell)*, Henry Darrow
(Lt. Manuel 'Manny' Quinlan), Anthony Zerbe *(Lt. KC Trench)*,
Farrah Fawcett *(Sue Ingham)*

Writer: Howard Rodman

Producer: Jerry Thorpe, Rita Dillon & Robert E. Thompson

First Broadcast: USA 12 September 1974 – 29 April 1977

Runtime: 45 episodes x 60 min & 2 x 120 min

DVD: Currently Unavailable

Hangdoggy faced ex-marine and LA cop Harry Orwell is retired with a bullet lodged in his back, and becomes a beach front-based private eye. Harry's always in pain from his injury and always broke because, most of the time, he doesn't even collect a fee, so he's forced to abandon his cranky old car and take the bus to make his investigations which is kind of inconvenient when trailing a suspect. Harry's next door neighbour is Farrah Fawcett, but Harry just doesn't seem interested in romance. More fool him.

weblinks

www.imdb.com/title/tt0070993/
www.youtube.com/watch?v=5eMyHO0Jd4s
www.tv.com/harry-o/show/819/summary.html
en.wikipedia.org/wiki/Harry_O

28. WITHOUT A TRACE

USA – BBC (Seven Seasons)

Cast: Anthony LaPaglia *(Jack Malone)*, Poppy Montgomery
(Samantha Spade), Enrique Murciano *(Danny Taylor)*, Eric Close

(Martin Fitzgerald), Marianne Jean-Baptiste *(Vivian Johnson)*
Writer: Hank Steinberg
Producers: Jonathan Littman, Hank Steinberg & Jerry Bruckheimer
First Broadcast (US): 26 September 2002 – 19 May 2009
Runtime: 160 plus episodes x 60 min
DVD: Warner Home Video 2005

At the start of every show, an individual is seen going about their business until they gradually fade away. Gone without a trace as they say. But no one can vanish completely without leaving some kind of clue, and that's where Jack Malone (Anthony LaPaglia) and his FBI unit come into play. Jack is a troubled man, with problems of his own, including in later series an unfortunate predilection to put on vast amounts of weight. I know there must be a joke in there somewhere, but can't think of it for the moment.

weblinks

www.imdb.com/title/tt0321021/
www.youtube.com/watch?v=CXAJif3MC6Q
www.tv.com/without-a-trace/show/7449/summary.html
en.wikipedia.org/wiki/Without_a_Trace
www.cbs.com/primetime/without_a_trace/
www.amazon.co.uk/Without-Trace-Complete-Season-DVD/dp/B0002GZA2K/

27. THE UNIT

USA – BRAVO (Four Seasons)
Cast: Dennis Haysbert *(Jonas Blane)*, Regina Taylor *(Molly Blane)*,
Audrey Marie Anderson *(Kim Brown)*, Robert Patrick *(Colonel Tom Ryan)*,
Max Martini *(Mack Gerhardt)*, Abby Brammell *(Tiffy Gerhardt)*,
Scott Foley *(Bob Brown)*
Writers: Eric L. Haney & David Mamet
Producers: Nicolas Bradley, Sharon Lee Watson, David Mamet,

Lynn Mamet, Vahan Moosekian & Shawn Ryan
First Broadcast (US): 7 March 2006 – 10 May 2009
Runtime: 69 episodes x 42 min
DVD: 20th Century Fox Home Entertainment 2007

This one definitely fits all the parameters for this book. Bad guys, spies, heroes, villains. The whole nine yards. No private eyes I'll admit, but no one, or no series, is perfect, though *The Unit* is pretty much so.

The show portrays the private and personal lives in Delta Force, the US Army top counterintelligence unit who kick arse and take names all over the world, and don't care who they kill or what they destroy to complete their missions. (Hurray, hurray for the USA, I say.) Although the titular boss of the unit is Colonel (later Brigadier General) Tom Ryan (Robert Patrick), like *Ultimate Force**, in fact, the guv'nor is a non-commissioned officer, Sergeant Major Jonas Blane, call sign Snake Doctor (Dennis Haysbert) whose comrades are known as Dirt Diver, Betty Blue (a bloke), Dog Patch, Hammerhead, Red Cap, and Whiplash. Man, these cats don't give a shit when they're on a mission, but at home they're all pretty much pussy whipped by their old women. Just like real life I reckon.

Four series have been made, and now the show is cancelled. Just like real life I reckon.

weblinks

www.imdb.com/title/tt0460690/
www.imdb.com/media/rm2139723520/tt0460690?slideshow=1
en.wikipedia.org/wiki/Without_a_Trace
www.tv.com/the-unit/show/33480/summary.html
www.amazon.co.uk/Unit-Season-Complete-DVD/dp/B000MTF0CW/

26. TAGGART

UK – ITV(Twenty Six Seasons)
Cast: Mark McManus *(Taggart)*, Blythe Duff *(DS Jackie Reid)*, Alex Norton *(DCI Burke)*, Colin McCredie *(DC Stuart Fraser)*, John Michie *(DI Robbie Ross)*
Writer: Glenn Chandler
Producers: Graeme Gordon & Eric Coulter
First Broadcast (UK): 6 September 1983 – Present
Runtime: 103 episodes x 60/120 min
DVD: Clear Vision Ltd 2007

Vying with *The Bill** as the longest running crime series in the UK (*Taggart* is the winner by a hair), the show actually began as a one-off three parter called *Killer*, set in the fictional Maryhill police station in the northern division of Glasgow, starred Mark McManus as Detective Chief Inspector Jim Taggart, a hard drinking, tough cop of the old school with a soft centre. His wife Jean (Harriet Buchan) had been wheelchair-bound for twenty plus years, and Taggart was her carer. When *Killer* turned out to be a success, a series was commissioned, and named after the chief cop, and is still going strong today. (The first episode was entitled *Dead Ringer*, and coincidentally the first episode of *The Sweeney**, back in the day, was called *Ringer*. Spooky.) Early in that first series, Taggart was assisted by DS Livingstone (Neil Duncan) who was replaced by Mike Jardine (James Macpherson) (Who, when I went to a party at ITN House, had a pee next to me in the gents. We didn't speak. It's not done). Jardine was too strait-laced for Taggart, but after McManus died in 1994, he took over as boss, although the title remained the same. When Jardine was murdered in 2002, DCI Matt Burke took over the squad where he remains to this day.

weblinks

www.imdb.com/title/tt0088621/
www.youtube.com/watch?v=Lb7NAJX2Uyl
www.tv.com/taggart/show/1407/summary.html
en.wikipedia.org/wiki/Taggart
www.amazon.co.uk/Taggart-Collection-DVD-42-discs/dp/B000V0NHNG/

25. STARSKY AND HUTCH

USA – BBC (Four Seasons)
Cast: Paul Michael Glaser *(Dave Starsky)*, David Soul *(Ken Hutchinson)*,
Antonio Fargas *(Huggy Bear)*, Bernie Hamilton *(Capt. Harold Dobey)*
Writer: William Blinn
Producers: Leonard Goldberg & Aaron Spelling
First Broadcast (US): 30 April 1975 – 15 May 1979
Runtime: 88 episodes x 60 min
DVD: Sony Pictures Home Entertainment 2006

Yet another cop show that changed the way we watched cop shows, and spawned books, toys and fashions for young men. It starred Paul Michael Glaser as Detective Dave Starsky, proud owner of a red 1974 Ford Torino with a go-faster stripe, and David Soul, as his partner Detective Ken Hutchinson who drove a beat up something or other. It was a bit homo-erotic at times, but no one cared.

There were car chases galore, gun fights up the wazoo, and the wonderful Antonio Fargas as jive talking, cool walking Huggy Bear, who was their main informant.

Soul turned out several terrible records at the time, whose titles I refuse to contemplate, like the big screen remake.

weblinks

www.imdb.com/title/tt0072567/
www.youtube.com/watch?v=GN1grF2rXpM
en.wikipedia.org/wiki/Starsky_and_Hutch
www.tv.com/starsky-and-hutch/show/81/summary.html
www.amazon.co.uk/Starsky-Hutch-1-4-Complete-DVD/dp/B000JLTE4S/

24. 24

USA – SKY ONE (Eight Seasons)
Cast: Kiefer Sutherland *(Jack Bauer)*, Mary Lynn Rajskub *(Chloe O'Brian)*, Carlos Bernard *(Tony Almeida)*
Writers: Robert Cochran & Joel Surnow
Producers: Paul Gadd, Brian Grazer & Howard Gordon
First Broadcast (US): 6 November 2001 – 24 May 2010
Runtime: 192 episodes x 45 min
DVD: 20th Century Fox 2009

When he's not banged up in a federal facility for some minor infringement of the law, Kiefer Sutherland plays Jack Bauer, a secret service agent for the Los Angeles based CTU (Counter Terrorist Unit) who, like Napoleon Solo before him in *The Man From U.N.C.L.E.**, is determined to make the world safe for the American way, Mom and apple pie. In the first series, Senator David Palmer (Dennis Haysbert from *The Unit**) is poised to become the first black American president, several years before there actually was one. But dirty work is afoot, an assassination is planned, and it seems that only Jack can save the day. Then his annoying daughter Kim (Elisha Cuthbert) goes missing and it seems that her life too is in danger. How I wish it had come to pass. The USP of the show was that it was made in twenty-four episodes, each one being one hour of the day that Jack doesn't eat, sleep, take a pee, or anything that normal people do in twenty-four hours. Mind you he's beaten to within an inch of his life, and doesn't turn a hair. (Or comb one for that matter.) Ridiculous, of course, but a massive success on both sides of the Atlantic, and a further six series were made, when Jack gets into ever more life-threatening scrapes.

weblinks

www.imdb.com/title/tt0285331/
www.imdb.com/media/rm872120832/tt0285331?slideshow=1
www.youtube.com/watch?v=_p_i_baiPvc
en.wikipedia.org/wiki/24_(TV_series)
www.tv.com/24/show/3866/summary.html
www.amazon.co.uk/24-Complete-Season-Plus-Redemption/dp/B0029NZSCQ/

23. SMITH

USA – ITV4 (One Season)

Cast: Ray Liotta *(Bobby Stevens)*, Virginia Madsen *(Hope Stevens)*, Simon Baker *(Jeff Breen)*, Jonny Lee Miller *(Tom)*, Franky G *(Joe Garcia)*, Amy Smart *(Annie)*, Chris Bauer *(Agent Dodd)*, Shohreh Aghdashloo *(Charlie)*

Writer: John Wells

Producer: Brooke Kennedy

First Broadcast (US): 19 September 2006 – 3 October 2006

Runtime: 7 episodes x 60 min

DVD: Currently Unavailable

And another one that dropped by the wayside. Just like *Heist**, same year, same small number of episodes before cancellation. Great show, but a tiny audience by US standards, hence the poor thing was put out of its misery. Ray Liotta played the lead role as Bobby Stevens, aka Smith, the leader of a gang of thieves always looking for the big score. The team were Tom (Jonny Lee Miller), head of logistics and Bobby's No 2, Joe (Franky G.) transport manager, Jeff (Simon Baker) armourer, Annie (Amy Smart) master of disguises, Charlie (Shohreh Aghdashloo. I bet he has fun phoning call centres) sort of architect of the robberies they plan. And then there's Virginia Madsen as Bobby's wife Hope. Presumably that springs eternal, as the gang planned a different robbery in each of the seven episodes, and only three actually appeared in the States. Pretty much *Heist** by another name as I said. ITV 4 and Hallmark both showed the series over here, but no DVD as I write. A great pity in my opinion, as both shows could have had more of a future.

The show's theme was *Show Me How to Live* by Audioslave. Put that into your MP3 player and smoke it.

weblinks

www.imdb.com/title/tt0805667/
www.youtube.com/watch?v=k-yhFcntJXU&feature=related
www.tv.com/smith/show/58081/summary.html?q=Smith&tag
en.wikipedia.org/wiki/Smith_(TV_series)

22. MURDER BAG

UK – ITV (Two Seasons)
Cast: Raymond Francis (Supt Tom Lockhart)
Writer: Glyn Davies
Producer: Barry Baker
First Broadcast (UK): 16 September 1957 – 1 April 1959
Runtime: 55 episodes x 30 min in Black and White
DVD: Currently Unavailable.

Golden age stuff, but sadly once again in shades of grey. *Murder Bag* introduced crime busting, snuff snorting (yes, snuff. I said it was golden age). Detective Superintendent Tom Lockhart (Raymond Francis) who carried a briefcase full of forensic equipment to murder scenes. (How times have changed. Look how much gear *CSI** have to hand. The bag contained seventy items, including tweezers and airtight jars. How Gil Grissom would have laughed!) The show was transmitted live, and, later in 1959, he became lead character in *Crime Sheet*, which I must confess I have absolutely no memory of. It was ITV again, Lockhart was now Chief Superintendent, and handled all sorts of cases, to much success, and he was transferred to Scotland Yard, and the hit show *No Hiding Place**.

weblinks

www.imdb.com/title/tt0165049/
en.wikipedia.org/wiki/No_Hiding_Place
www.tv.com/murder-bag/show/62291/summary.html

21. NEW TRICKS

UK – BBC1 (Seven Seasons – an eighth in the making for 2011)
Cast: Alun Armstrong (Brian Lane), Amanda Redman
(Det Supt Sandra Pullman), Dennis Waterman (Gerry Standing),
James Bolam (Jack Halford)
Writers: Nigel McCrery & Roy Mitchell
Producer: Tom Sherry

First Broadcast (UK): 1 April 2004 – Present
Runtime: 55 episodes x 60 min (+ 8 still to come)
DVD: 2Entertain Video 2005 DVD BBC

They don't make 'em like this anymore. Actually they do of course, as at the time of writing *New Tricks* is number one on the BBC1 charts, and keeps coming back for more. More like they don't make cops like the three main men anymore. Old dicks brought in from the cold to investigate just that. Cold cases that no one else is interested in. The three lead actors are: Alun Armstrong as Brian Lane, James Bolam as Jack Halford and Dennis Waterman as Gerry Standing. And these three sure can pick big shows. Armstrong has been in more series than I've had hot dinners, Bolam starred in hits like *The Likely Lads* and *Whatever Happened*, etc., and *When the Boat Comes In*, and Waterman tops them both with *Just William, The Sweeney** and *Minder**, plus maybe a dozen more. Also starring is Amanda Redman as Detective Superintendent Sandra Pullman in charge of UCOS (Unsolved Crime and Open Case Squad), and Susan Jameson as Brian Lane's long suffering wife (Yes, another one.) Interestingly enough she was one of Bolam's love interests in *WTBCI* and latterly in real life, his wife.

So what's made it such a smash hit? Simple – chemistry. The three old pros work together like a well-oiled machine. Lane is a bit deranged, and an alcoholic who has Asperger's Syndrome. Standing is an old roué, with three wives, and countless female offspring who he tries to keep happy, and Halford's wife was killed in a hit-and-run accident, then buried in his back garden, to where he often retires to discuss cases with her spirit.

Beautifully scripted, with just enough comedy to offset the seriousness of some of the cases, it certainly deserves a higher rating, but sadly, the last series began to show a little tiredness around the edges. It's a heavy schedule to make shows like this one, and the blokes aren't getting any younger.

weblinks

www.imdb.com/title/tt0362357/
www.youtube.com/watch?v=pwdh46eHUC8
www.tv.com/new-tricks/show/17776/summary.html
en.wikipedia.org/wiki/New_Tricks_(TV_series)
www.amazon.co.uk/New-Tricks-Complete-BBC-DVD/dp/B0006PTYP6/

20. MIDSOMER MURDERS

UK – ITV (Thirteen Seasons)
Cast: John Nettles *(DCI Tom Barnaby)*, Jane Wymark *(Joyce Barnaby)*,
Barry Jackson *(Dr Bullard)*, Laura Howard *(Cully Barnaby)*
Writer: Caroline Graham
Producers: Brian True-May & Ian Strachan
First Broadcast (UK): 23 March 1997 – Present
Runtime: 75 episodes x 120 min
DVD: Acorn Media 2009

Oh to be in Midsomer now that April's here. Or any other time of the year for that matter. Actually no. For all its rural beauty, the county has hidden depths. Quite often six feet under for a number of its inhabitants, by all manner of strange and vicious means. Enter stage left, the imposing figure of Detective Chief Inspector Tom Barnaby, once the athletic *Bergerac**, but now a chunkier, slower moving individual, still capable of dampening the underwear of ladies of a certain age.

Most often when the call comes that another citizen of Badger's Drift or Midsomer Worthy has bitten the dust, Joyce, his long suffering wife (Jane Wymark, daughter of Patrick) is about to dish up a meal, or go shopping for a new suit for hubby, or catch a play at the local rep, or just trying to get a good night's sleep. Thus the Inspector, with one of long term sidekicks (Detective Sergeant Troy – Daniel Casey, Detective Sergeant Scott – John Hopkins, Detective Constable Jones – Jason Hughes), gets on the trail of the culprit(s) amid a raft of herrings so red they would put stop lights to shame.

But of course right always wins, and Barnaby is triumphant, and able to make one last wry crack as the credits roll, and the gentle theme tune closes the show.

The show became famous (notorious?) for being a pension for any silly old luvvies to drag their weary carcasses out of their bath chairs and make one more appearance on prime time TV. Don't knock it. You'll be old yourself one day.

Nettles has decided to leave the show, but it will continue, but who'll be the lead is not known at present. Adapted from the novels of Caroline Graham.

weblinks

www.imdb.com/title/tt0118401/
www.tv.com/midsomer-murders/show/4941/summary.html

19.   MIAMI VICE

USA – BBC1 (Five Seasons)
Cast: Don Johnson *(Detective James Crockett)*,
Philip Michael Thomas *(Detective Ricardo Tubbs)*, Edward James Olmos
(Lieutenant Martin Castillo), Saundra Santiago *(Detective Gina Calabrese)*,
Olivia Brown *(Detective Trudy Joplin)*, Michael Talbott *(Detective Stan Switek)*
Writer: Anthony Yerkovich
Producers: Michael Mann & Richard Brams
First Broadcast (US): 28 September 1984 – 25 January 1990
Runtime: 108 episodes x 60 min 3 episodes x 120 min (BBC1 1985 – 1990)
DVD: Universal 2007

Sometimes a TV series or film arrives that changes the look of the world.
Miami Vice was one such. Before Crockett & Tubbs hit the small screen
how many men sported designer stubble, wore pastel coloured trousers
and pushed the sleeves of their jackets, worn over silk T-shirts, up to their
elbows? Not many I'll be bound. But within a few weeks of the first episode
airing, thousands would. Like *CSI Miami**, twenty years later, the programme
set out to make the city seem as glamorous and glitzy as possible, but
unlike *CSI** the crimes were mostly drug related and the two heroes worked
undercover most of the time. Although, with the way they acted, I'm
surprised everyone in town didn't realise they were cops from the word go.
Not exactly keeping a low profile, Detective James 'Sonny' Crockett (Don
Johnson) lived on a houseboat called St Vitus Dance with an alligator named
Elvis. A sure way to stay under the radar. Tubbs meanwhile was not quite so
flash, but nearly. He arrived in Miami to flush out the gangster who killed
his brother. Hot wheels: Ferrari Spiders or Testarossas, hot babes, and the
latest dance tunes made *Miami Vice* the must see for red blooded young
men at the time. And Crockett & Tubbs posters decorated the walls of many
teenage girls, as they listened to the hit theme by Jan Hammer. In fact, the
show was shot in superb style, with the use of colour unprecedented.

Guest stars were numerous, as celebs wanted to climb on the bandwagon,
and included Little Richard, James Brown, Phil Collins, Ted Nugent and The
Fat Boys, which just goes to show how times change. Who would care about

them now? But at the time, *MTV* was hot, and cop shows were hot. Combine the two and what you got was the hottest thing on the box. It looks dated now, but still hits the nostalgia button for viewers of a certain age.

Forget the 2006 remake for the big screen.

weblinks

www.imdb.com/title/tt0086759/
en.wikipedia.org/wiki/Miami_Vice
www.tv.com/miami-vice/show/544/summary.html
www.amazon.co.uk/Miami-Vice-Complete-Collection-DVD/dp/B000SLW43M/

18. LAW & ORDER / SPECIAL VICTIMS UNIT CRIMINAL INTENT / TRIAL BY JURY

USA – BBC/CH5

LAW & ORDER (Twenty Seasons)

Cast: S. Epatha Merkerson *(Lt. Anita Van Buren),* Sam Waterston *(Executive ADA Jack McCoy),* Jerry Orbach *(Detective Lennie Briscoe),* Steven Hill *(DA Adam Schiff)*

Writer: Dick Wolf

Producer: Dick Wolf

First Broadcast (US): 13 September 1990 – 24 May 2010

Runtime: 456 episodes x 60 min

SPECIAL VICTIMS UNIT (Eleven Seasons)

Cast: Christopher Meloni *(Detective Elliot Stabler),* Mariska Hargitay *(Detective Olivia Benson),* Richard Belzer *(Detective John Munch),* Dann Florek *(Captain Donald Cragen),* Ice-T *(Detective Odafin 'Fin' Tutuola)*

Writer: Dick Wolf

Producers: David DeClerque, Ted Kotcheff & Dick Wolf

First Broadcast (US): 20 September 1999 – Present

Runtime 248 episodes x 60 min

CRIMINAL INTENT (Nine Seasons)

Cast: Kathryn Erbe *(Detective Alexandra Eames),* Vincent D'Onofrio *(Detective Robert Goren),* Jamey Sheridan *(Captain James Deakins),* Courtney B. Vance *(ADA Ron Carver),* Leslie Hendrix *(Dr Elizabeth Rodgers)*

Writers: Rene Balcer & Dick Wolf

Producers: Rene Balcer, John L. Roman, Peter Jankowski & Dick Wolf

First Broadcast (US): 7 October 2001 – Present

Runtime: 187 episodes x 43 min

TRIAL BY JURY (One Season)

Cast: Bebe Neuwirth *(ADA Tracey Kibre)*, Amy Carlson *(ADA Kelly Gaffney)*, Kirk Acevedo *(DA Arthur Branch)*, Scott Cohen *(Detective Chris Ravell)*

Writers: Chris Levinson, Walon Green & David Wilcox

Producers: Tony Phelan & Dick Wolf

First Broadcast (US): 3 March 2005 – 21 January 2006

Runtime: 13 episodes x 42 min

DVD: Universal 2008

The original American *Law & Order* kicked off in 1991 starring George Dzundza as Detective Sergeant Max Greevey, and Christopher Noth as Detective Mike Logan. Since then, cops have come and gone on a regular basis, probably the most memorable being the late Jerry Orbach as Detective Lennie Briscoe, with a way with wisecracks that was so dry as to be dust like. He is sadly missed.

The format was as follows: Half the show was the crime and capture of the suspect (or perps as they love to call them). The second half was the trial run by Assistant District Attorney Jack McCoy (Sam Waterston) and his various glamorous assistants to the Assistant DA, under the watchful eye of District Attorney Arthur Branch, played by Fred Dalton Thompson.

In 1999 came *Law & Order: Special Victims Unit,* with Christopher Meloni as Detective Elliot Stabler, Detective John Munch from *Homicide** once again played by Richard Belzer, and Mariska Hargity (Jayne Mansfield's daughter) as Detective Olivia Benson. This series concentrated on sex crimes, and at times could be quite horrifying.

My favourite of the series came along in 2001. *Law & Order: Criminal Intent* starred the wonderful Vincent D'Onofrio as Detective Robert Goren, a mixture of Columbo and Einstein. He seems to speak most languages, and knows more or less everything about everything. His partner is the small, but perfectly formed (and I mean perfectly) Detective Alexandra Eames played by Kathryn Erbe. If you're going to be nicked, this is the babe to do it. Finally, and least successfully, came *Law & Order: Trial by Jury* with Bebe Neuwirth as Assistant District Attorney Tracey Kibre. It was shown on ITV3 in 2006, but made little or no impact.

Music by Mike Post

weblinks

http://en.wikipedia.org/wiki/Law_and_Order_franchise

Law and Order:
www.imdb.com/title/tt0098844/
www.tv.com/law-and-order/show/180/summary.html

Law and Order SVU:
www.imdb.com/title/tt0203259/
www.tv.com/law-and-order-special-victims-unit/show/334/summary.html
www.amazon.co.uk/Law-Order-First-Seasons-SVU/dp/

Law and Order CI:
www.imdb.com/title/tt0275140/
www.tv.com/law-and-order-criminal-intent/show/1381/summary.html

17.   HEIST

USA – SATELLITE (One Season)
Cast: Marika Dominczyk *(Lola)*, Dougray Scott *(Mickey O'Neil)*,
Michele Hicks *(Amy Sykes)*
Writers: Mark Cullen & Robb Cullen
Producers: Mark Cullen & Robb Cullen
First Broadcast (US): 22 March 2006 – 19 April 2006
Runtime: 7 episodes x 60 min Satellite: 2006
DVD: Currently Unavailable

A blink and you'll miss it series, as Mickey O'Neil (Dougray Scott) plans the biggest jewel heist in history, of three jewellery stores on Rodeo Drive during Academy Awards week, whilst Hollywood cop Amy Sykes (Michele Hicks), lead detective for the LAPD's Robbery Division, tries to figure out what's happening, and bust O'Neil's gang of expert thieves. So low were the ratings in the USA that it was cancelled as soon as it started and the last two episodes were never shown. It was possible to catch it on one of those channels way up the digi box, but sadly no sign of a DVD. Pity, because I thought it was very good.

16. THE GOLD ROBBERS

UK – ITV (One Season)
Cast: Peter Vaughan *(DCS Cradock)*, Artro Morris *(DS Tommy Thomas)*,
Richard Leech *(Richard Bolt)*
Writer: John Hawkesworth
Producer: John Hawkesworth
First Broadcast (UK): 6 June 1969 – 29 August 1969
Runtime: 13 episodes x 60 min in Black and White
DVD: Currently Unavailable

This really was a crime show highlight from 1969. I was selling insurance for a living at the time, and Friday night was collection night, and what a downer that was. *The Gold Robbers* was the only thing to look forward to during that blighted period of my life. Peter Vaughan starred as Detective Chief Superintendent Cradock, determined to track down the gang who stole five and a half million quid in gold from an aircraft. Supporting roles went to the likes of George Cole, Nicholas Ball, Roy Dotrice and Alfred Lynch.

15. BIG BREADWINNER HOG

UK – ITV (One Season)
Cast: Peter Egan *(Hog)*, Alan Browning *(Izzard)*, Donald Burton *(Ackerman)*, Timothy West *(Lennox)*, Rosemary McHale *(Joanna Edgeworth)*, James Hunter *(Raymond Balls)*, David Leland *(Grange)*
Writer: Robin Chapman

Producer: Robin Chapman
First Broadcast (UK): 11 April 1969 – 30 May 1969
Runtime: 8 episodes x 60 min
DVD: Network 2007

A bona fide video nasty in its day, *Big Breadwinner Hog* starred Peter Egan as the nasty face of gangland London. He literally wants to live high on the hog, and is determined to let nothing stand in the way of his ambition to be top dog. (It's all hogs and dogs.) But he doesn't get it all his own way and ultraviolence ensues. In fact, when the first episode was shown one Friday night, there were so many complaints that the show hit the Saturday papers, and ITV had to issue an apology. In fact it was great fun, and I must pick up the DVD soon.

weblinks

www.imdb.com/title/tt0063870/
en.wikipedia.org/wiki/Big_Breadwinner_Hog
www.tv.com/big-breadwinner-hog/show/75981/summary.html
www.amazon.co.uk/Big-Breadwinner-Hog-Complete-Spindoe/dp/B000LXHJMI

14. BOOMTOWN

USA (Two Seasons)
Cast: Donnie Wahlberg *(Detective Joel Stevens)*, Neal McDonough
(David McNorris), Mykelti Williamson *(Detective Bobby 'Fearless' Smith)*,
Gary Basaraba *(Officer Ray Hechler)*, Lana Parrilla *(Teresa Ortiz)*,
Jason Gedrick *(Officer Tom Turcotte)*
Writer: Graham Yost
Producers: Jon Avnet & Graham Yost
First Broadcast (US): 29 September 2002 – 28 December 2003
Runtime: 24 episodes x 45 min
DVD: Lionsgate 2004

Boomtown's producers illustrate perfectly how to make a fabulous first series, be commissioned for a second, and ruin it so badly it was chopped off at the knees. The premise of the first series was to show one crime from several points of view. Time skips, characters disappear and reappear, and, although it sounds strange, it really worked. You really have to see it, and I recommend you do. Then it came back as a straightforward cop show, and it flopped. Donnie Wahlberg starred.

weblinks

www.imdb.com/title/tt0319960/ www.youtube.com/watch?v=TX8UkujMuyY
www.tv.com/boomtown/show/9581/summary.html
en.wikipedia.org/wiki/Boomtown_(TV_series)
www.amazon.co.uk/Boomtown-Season-One-Region-NTSC/dp/B00005JMMT/

13. M SQUAD

USA – ITV (Three Seasons)

Cast: Lee Marvin *(Detective Lt. Frank Ballinger)*,
Ed Herlihy *(Opening Announcer)*, Paul Newlan *(Police Capt. Grey)*

Writers: Jack Laird, Joel Murcott & Stuart Jerome

Producers: John Larkin, Maxwell Shane & Richard Lewis

First Broadcast (US): 20 September 1957 – 28 June 1960

Runtime: 117 episodes x 30 min in Black and White

DVD: Universal/Timeless Video2008

(includes *The Music from M Squad* **Sony/BMG CD)**

One of the daddies of them all, *M Squad* starred Lee Marvin as tough Chicago cop Lieutenant Frank Ballinger, head of a plain clothes homicide detail (M, stands for Murder you see) who pull no punches as they police the streets of the windy city. A huge hit at the time on both sides of the Atlantic, it was violent and uncompromising for the period, and set up Marvin for the parts he later played on the big screen as numero uno hard man. In fact Ballinger could have been the template for Marvin's greatest role (in my opinion, which is all that matters here), as Parker in *Point Blank*.

Marvin narrates the stories as he rushes around the town hunting the bad guys, toting all manner of ordnance, including machine guns, and there are some memorable shoot outs and car chases. Plus there was a great score, with the best remembered theme composed by Count Basie. It's interesting to note (at least to me) that Robert Altman cut his directorial teeth on some episodes.

I got an imported DVD from America which runs to 2,866 minutes, and was worth every penny it cost me, which let me tell you was a lot.

12. HILL STREET BLUES

USA – ITV/CH4 (Seven Seasons)

Cast: Daniel J Travanti *(Capt. Frank Furillo)*, Taurean Blacque
(Det Neal Washington), Bruce Weitz *(Sgt Mick Belker)*, Joe Spano
(Det Henry Goldblume), Kiel Martin *(Officer John 'JD' LaRue)*,
Betty Thomas *(Sgt Lucy Bates)*, Veronica Hamel *(Joyce Davenport)*,
Charles Haid *(Officer Andrew Renko)*, Michael Warren
(Officer Robert 'Bobby' Hill), James Sikking *(Lt. Howard Hunter)*
Writers: Steven Bochco & Jeffrey Lewis
Producers: Scott Brazil, Gregory Hoblit & Steven Bochco
First Broadcast (US): 15 January 1981 – 12 May 1987
Runtime: 146 episodes x 60min
DVD: Channel 4 2006

A brilliant ensemble cast including Daniel J Travanti (Captain Frank Furillo),
Bruce Weitz (Detective Mick Belker, who used to bite those he arrested and
growl like a dog), James B. Sikking (gung ho, and gun crazy SWAT team
leader Lieutenant Howard Hunter), Veronica Hamel (sexy defence lawyer
who later marries Furillo, Joyce Davenport) and Charles Haid (cowboy boot
wearing good old boy Officer Andy Renko) thrust Stephen Bochco's tales of
the Hill Street police precinct in the unnamed city (Chicago played host to
the location shots), where comedy and tragedy often wore the same hat,
into a critical success, but not a big hit in the ratings. A memorable theme
tune once again introduced our heroes and heroines every week, and
Sergeant Phil Easterhaus' plea at the end of roll call 'And hey, let's be careful
out there,' has gone down as one of the great lines in TV history.

Oddly enough it was *Hill Street Blues* that got me my first video recorder;
back when it started I was offered a job driving a loser heavy metal band
called *720* (apparently the speed that the sound barrier is broken). The show

had just started and I took the job on the condition that the manager paid for the hire of a VCR. He agreed. Blimey, the thing was the size of a suitcase, top loaded, with piano keys that you needed the strength of ten men to depress. I think it had a remote control that was actually connected to the machine by a thick cable, but I might be dreaming, because my memories of those days are rather patchy. Neither the job nor the band lasted very long, which was probably good news for music lovers, but at least I got into the trendy video age. What a geezer!

weblinks

www.imdb.com/title/tt0081873/
en.wikipedia.org/wiki/Hill_Street_Blues
www.tv.com/hill-street-blues/show/269/summary.html
www.amazon.co.uk/Hill-Street-Blues-1-DVD/dp/B000E1P2VM/

11. PROSPECTS

UK – CH4/ITV (One Season)
Cast: Gary Olsen *(Pincy)*, Brian Bovell *(Billy)*,
Chrissie Cotterill *(Mona)*, GB Money *(Marv)*,
Mike Savage *(Del)*, Ben Howard *(Detective Sergeant Halforth)*
Writer: Alan Janes
Producers: John Crome, Peter Ellis, Bernard Rose
First Broadcast (UK): 19 February 1986 – 7 May 1986
Runtime: 12 episodes x 60 min
DVD: Currently Unavailable

From Euston Films in the mid-eighties came this hybrid of *Minder** and *Only Fools and Horses*, complete with a vomit yellow van in the first episode. (Not a three-wheeler, but a Bedford, which was simply a horrible Vauxhall Viva with a box on the back.) The show was set in Docklands (particularly the Isle of Dogs) pre-gentrification, when it was still an Enterprise Zone, and Canary Wharf was just a dream. (In fact it is a location in one episode, and the building is red brick, and only a couple of storeys high.) The series starred the late Gary Olsen, who sadly died far too young, as Pincy, and Brian Bovell as Billy, a salt and pepper pair of duckers and divers looking for a break. Something with prospects in fact. The pilot kicked off with the postman delivering giros to the lads, who then have to pay a fortnight's worth of debts (how well I remember) leaving them just enough for a pint and a pie, before beginning the whole routine again. They start businesses, left right and centre, conning their mates, and any pretty girl they manage to pull and get to lend them a tenner, while at the same time trying to prevent the aforementioned motor being repossessed. Though why anyone would want it in the first place beats me. (It's later replaced by an Austin hearse that constantly breaks down, but what these two jokers don't realise is that the registration mark of AAA 10C was probably worth several thousand pounds, even in those days.) And they really were the days, when a VCR cost three hundred quid, and the posters on the wall were of Grace Jones, Sylvester Stallone as Rocky and *Bob Marley and The Wailers*.

A further highlight of the series was Chrissie Cotterill playing Mona, Pincy's dopey girlfriend, with possibly the best looking arse on the Island.

Hazel O'Connor makes a guest appearance in one episode, and I wonder whatever happened to her. Appearing in the same segment was GB Money as Marv her manager. Otherwise known as Zoot Money from the marvellous Big Roll Band and Dantilian's Chariot.

Then, like a blast from another life, Ben Howard plays the nasty Detective Sergeant (later Detective Inspector) Halforth. I knew Ben when he was known as 'Mr Benjy' the king of skateboards, and I worked in his warehouse building the bloody things. Boy, I could tell you some tales about that episode in my life, but I think it's best to draw a veil over the whole experience.

The theme was written by Ray Dorset from Mungo Jerry, and performed by Made in England and the writer himself. Mint copy on 7' vinyl? Six quid to you Guv'nor.

I got a DVD of the series on TV-memories, which looked like it was copied off UK TV, and came complete without title, cast list, or any information whatsoever. Street legal? Who knows, unlikely but it fits the type of show it contains perfectly.

weblinks

www.imdb.com/title/tt0134259/
en.wikipedia.org/wiki/Prospects_(TV_series)
www.tv.com/prospects/show/20886/summary.html
tv-nostalgia.com/detailsprospects.htm
www.amazon.co.uk/Prospects-Complete-3DVD-Gary-Olsen/dp/B000QRO6X4/

IN REVERSE ORDER AS ALWAYS:

10. LUTHER

UK – BBC1 (One Season)
Cast: Steven Mackintosh *(DCI Ian Reed)*, Warren Brown *(DS Justin Ripley)*, Indira Varma *(Zoe Luther)*, Paul McGann *(Mark North)*, Ruth Wilson *(Alice Morgan)*, Idris Elba *(DCI John Luther)*, Saskia Reeves *(DSU Rose Teller)*
Writer: Neil Cross
Producers: Idris Elba, Phillippa Giles, Leila Kirkpatrick & Katie Swinden
First Broadcast (UK): 4 May 2010 – 8 June 2010
Runtime: 6 episodes x 60 min
DVD: 2Entertain 2010

The show is as mad as a box of frogs, and has had severe criticism for being so unrealistic, but surely there's enough realism in the world as it is.

Luther, played by Idris Elba (Stringer Bell in *The Wire**) is a maverick cop (yes, another one) who's been suspended because a suspect took a long walk off a short gangway several floors up and ended up in a coma (and yes Luther helped him on his way, before you ask) with a long suffering wife (yes, I know) who actually isn't suffering much, as she's slung him out and taken up with a fancy man. (Christ, in all my years I've never used that expression before.) Anyway, when Luther cottons on, he destroys a door in her lovely house. (She's a humanitarian lawyer, you understand, but it doesn't mean she doesn't get very well paid.) Then, next day, when something doesn't go right at work, he destroys his office desk. Excellent stuff.

Meanwhile, he's being plagued by a psychopathic killer who shot her mum and dad, and then the dog, where she hid the murder weapon. Sorry, Luther, you may be top cop, but I worked that out before you did. Nyah, nyah, nyah. The killer is actually extremely horny, with a wonderful overbite. Of course Luther breaks into her flat without a warrant looking for evidence and, when he finds it, throws it in the river. Like I said, mad as a box of frogs. In fact it gets madder, as by episode three, Luther and the psycho are having a sort of unconsummated love affair.

In fact I have now seen the whole series and it does get crazier. If you haven't seen it, get the DVD. You won't be sorry.

weblinks

www.imdb.com/title/tt1474684/
www.youtube.com/watch?v=m_Qg1pQSOa0
www.tv.com/luther/show/77922/summary.html
en.wikipedia.org/wiki/Luther_(TV_series)
www.amazon.co.uk/Luther-DVD-Ruth-Wilson/dp/B003EELZH6/

9.   THE KILL POINT

USA – BRAVO (One Season)

Cast: Steve Cirbus *(Deke Quinlan)*, John Leguizamo *(Mr Wolf)*, Michael Hogan *(Hawk)*, Donnie Wahlberg *(Horst Cali)*, Adam Cantor *(Rocko)*, Geoffrey Cantor *(Abe Shelton)*, Jeremy Davidson *(Mr Rabbit)*, Jennifer Ferrin *(Chloe)*, Frank Grillo *(Mr Pig)*, Wayne Kasserman *(Tonray)*, JD Williams *(Cat)*, Ryan Sands *(Leroy)*

Writers: James DeMonaco & Josh Trank

Producers: Jay Benson, Todd Harthan, Bill Hill & Randy Nelson

First Broadcast (US): 22 July 2007 – 26 August 2007

Runtime: 1 episode x 85 min 7 episodes x 40 min

DVD: Lionsgate Home Entertainment 2008

This one didn't even get a major channel outing when it appeared over here in 2009. Shame on the commissioning editors of BBC and ITV drama, as it knocked most of that year's terrestrial offerings into the proverbial cocked hat. The series is split into one eighty-five minute, and seven forty minute episodes, each one, apart from the first, depicting an hour into a botched bank raid by a squad of disenfranchised soldiers led by 'Mr Wolf', played in fine style by John Leguizamo. (Just like *24*, we have to allow for ad breaks, so real time is never quite that.) The location is the Three Rivers Trust Bank in Pittsburgh, Pennsylvania. The rest of the gang are only known as Mr Mouse, Mr Rabbit, Mr Cat and Mr Pig.

Check Mr Wolf's opening lines as he and the gang, hooded, black mackintoshed, and armed to the teeth, burst through the bank's doors. 'As you rightly assume, this is a bank robbery, OK? All I ask of you is to sit still and breathe and be silent. I don't want to hurt you. All I want is the money. Don't stand up and dance.'

When the robbery falls apart as they leave the premises, and a federal agent is shot dead, the gang retreat back into the bank, holding staff and customers as hostages. Enter Donnie Wahlberg as Horst Cali (crazy name, crazy guy), hostage negotiator and all round kick arse tough cop who takes no nonsense from Wolf.

On the other hand, Wolf takes no nonsense from Cali and the authorities, and at one point leaves the bank to make an impassioned plea on behalf of his soldier buddies who came back from Iraq suffering wounds both physical and mental. As he strips to expose his tattoos and scars, suddenly the mood of the crowd of sightseers, rubberneckers, and thrill freaks outside the bank changes, and the cops have to abandon their plans to assault the building.

This was a great show but, like so many others, any chance of a sequel was nixed, owing to the small audience that it got Stateside.

weblinks

www.imdb.com/title/tt0862593/
www.tv.com/the-kill-point/show/74619/summary.html
en.wikipedia.org/wiki/The_Kill_Point
www.amazon.co.uk/Kill-Point-DVD-John-Leguizamo/dp/B0014XVTFC/

8. PUBLIC EYE

UK – ITV (Seven Seasons)
Cast: Alfred Burke *(Frank Marker)*
Writer: Roger Marshall
Producer: Michael Chapman
First Broadcast (UK): 23 January 1965 – 7 April 1975
Runtime: 74 episodes x 60 min in Black and White
& 26 episodes x 60 min in Colour

DVD: Network 2004

Many years ago, when I was a young man and hardly been kissed, Saturday night was enlivened by the appearance of a crime series called Public Eye.

It went through many changes until 1975 when it finished, *and* I'd possibly been kissed too much.

What I liked about it then, and still do, was the dour PI of the title: Frank Marker, a total loser, who made losers like I was then, feel that it was possible to lose and still succeed. Confused? Don't be. Remember, this is my book, and if I want to make a detour off memory lane then I will.

The first series was set in London where Marker sets up shop in a seedy back street office, and takes on hopeless cases where payment is scarce if it exists at all. Lugubrious to the extreme, Marker wears his shabby suit and dirty mac like a knight with rusty armour.

Later he relocates to Birmingham, then, after a spell in prison for a crime he didn't commit, he ends up in Brighton with a nice landlady (Helen Mortimer played by Pauline Delaney) who desperately wants to care for him. Fruitlessly as it goes. Funnily enough, one episode was titled *They Go off in the End, Like Fruit*. Sadly it did go off, and nothing like it was seen again until *Hazell**.

weblinks

www.imdb.com/title/tt0058842/
www.youtube.com/watch?v=Lt6xRqf3TE0
en.wikipedia.org/wiki/Public_Eye_(TV_series)
www.tv.com/public-eye/show/11931/summary.html
www.amazon.co.uk/Public-Eye-Complete-1969-DVD/dp/B000163WIU/

7. CSI: CRIME SCENE INVESTIGATION
CSI: LAS VEGAS
CSI: MIAMI
CSI: NEW YORK

USA – CH5

CSI: Las Vegas (Eleven Seasons)

Cast: Marg Helgenberger *(Catherine Willows)*, George Eads *(Nick Stokes)*, Paul Guilfoyle *(Captain Jim Brass)*, Eric Szmanda *(Dr Al Robbins)*, William

Petersen *(Gil Grissom)*, Laurence Fishburne *(Dr Raymond Langston)*
First Broadcast (US): 6 October 2000 – Present
Runtime: 229 episodes x 45 min

CSI: NY (Seven Seasons)
Cast: Gary Sinise *(Detective Mac Taylor)*, Melina Kanakaredes
(Detective Stella Bonasera), Hill Harper *(Dr Sheldon Hawkes)*,
Eddie Cahill *(Detective Don Flack)*
First Broadcast (US): 22 September 2004 – Present
Runtime: 140 episodes x 45 min

CSI: Miami (Nine Seasons)
Cast: David Caruso *(Lt. Horatio Caine)*, Emily Proctor *(Calleigh Duquesne)*,
Adam Rodriguez *(Eric Delko)*, Rex Linn *(Detective Frank Tripp)*
First Broadcast (US): 23 September 2002 – Present
Writers: Ann Donahue, Carol Mendelsohn & Anthony E. Zuiker
Producers: Jerry Bruckheimer, Ann Donahue, Jonathan Littman,
Carol Mendelsohn & Anthony E. Zuiker
Runtime: 191 epidodes x 45 min
DVD: Momentum Pictures Numerous Release Dates

Probably the most successful TV franchise ever; the three *CSI* series have run
for over ten years and more than 500 episodes. And do you know, I think I've
seen every one, some more than once, and even bought some DVD box sets
back in the day. A glutton for punishment you might say. That's days of my
life I'll never get back. Not at all. Though recently not as hot as it used to be,
CSI still presses most of the right buttons for me.

It all began on CBS TV on October 6th 2000, and new episodes are still being
made as I write.

Created by Anthony E. Zuiker and produced by Jerry Bruckheimer, all three
series show people dying in the most preposterous fashions, and the three
teams solving the mysteries week after week using the latest forensic
techniques, and at the same time looking wonderfully glamorous as they
go about their grisly tasks.

The original *CSI* starred William Petersen as Dr Gilbert 'Gil' Grissom as the
night shift supervisor for the Las Vegas CSI unit. His appearance sparked my

interest from episode one as he starred in two of my favourite films: *Red Dragon*, which I still think is the best adaptation of a Thomas Harris novel, where he was the FBI agent on the trail of Hannibal Lecter, and *To Live And Die In LA*, where he played a corrupt cop. Just brilliant. Then he seemed to disappear, only to come back as the insect loving scientist in *CSI*. Sadly, he left in 2008 to be replaced by Laurence Fishburne as Dr Raymond 'Ray' Langston. He's good, but not really good enough to fill Petersen's shoes. A fact of which Petersen himself is well aware, as I read an interview with him last year in *The Telegraph* when he would make very little comment about his replacement or the way the series has gone.

Then, in 2002, along came *CSI:Miami*, this one billed as created by Zuiker, Carol Mendelsohn and Ann Donahue. There's plenty of female action in Las Vegas, but Miami takes the biscuit. The city comes across as just one glamorous playground with little sign of the senior citizens I saw on my one and only visit. The whole show is crumpet central with enough gratuitous shots of young women in swimsuits and dresses so skimpy as to be almost invisible. No complaints from me there. But the one and only true star of this particular series is David Caruso. Dear David. Always a favourite of mine since his appearance in *NYPD Blue**. He got a bad rap when he quit that show and went to Hollywood to become a star on the big screen. Never happened. But the handful of films he made during that fallow time are amongst my favourites, mostly seeing him driving around the midwest of the USA in perfectly restored muscle cars robbing banks and killing folks.

In the series, Caruso plays Lieutenant Horatio 'H' Caine, head of the Miami-Dade crime lab, and interestingly enough a former NYPD Homicide Detective, which is exactly what he played in *NYPD Blue**. He had two signature trademarks in the show. One is the sunglasses action, when, as he contemplates the latest corpse to come his way, he removes them slowly, then just as slowly replaces them on his nose. Round my house, bets are laid as to when this dramatic conceit will take place. Then, usually when the bins are off, he makes some profound statement about the cause of death, life, and the whole ball of wax. Brilliant.

The third leg of the franchise is *CSI:NY* starring Gary Sinise as CSI Detective First Grade: Mac Taylor. This series has never gone down so well with me, as

Sinise plays the copper closer to Jesus than I find comfortable. His character is always making pious statements that just don't ring true. David Caruso he ain't.

Music plays a big part in the three series. The instrumental for the first *CSI:Las Vegas* has been replaced by *Who are You* by The Who. *Won't get Fooled Again* for *CSI:Miami* and *Baba O'Riley* for *CSI:NY*, both also by The Who, which must have been a right little earner over the years. Other artists to feature include The Wallflowers, Marilyn Manson, John Mayer and many others who enhance the plot. As it goes, sometimes too much, as in common with so many other US TV series, some ditty is played over dramatic scenes often for no purpose, and unfortunately this habit is also becoming common on this side of the Atlantic.

Every series of all three shows has appeared on DVD with bundles of extras including comic outtakes, which I refuse to watch. The last thing I want to see is David Caruso dropping his sunglasses.

weblinks

CSI (Eleven Seasons): www.imdb.com/title/tt0247082/
www.tv.com/csi/show/19/summary.html

CSI NY(Six Seasons): www.imdb.com/title/tt0395843/
www.tv.com/csi-ny/show/24125/summary.html

CSI Miami (Eight Seasons): www.imdb.com/title/tt0313043/
www.tv.com/csi-miami/show/8460/summary.html

www.youtube.com/results?search_query=csi+opening+credits
en.wikipedia.org/wiki/CSI:_Crime_Scene_Investigation
www.amazon.co.uk/s/ref=nb_sb_noss?url=search-alias%3Ddvd&field-keywords=csi

6. NYPD BLUE

USA – C4 (Twelve Seasons)
Cast: Dennis Franz *(Det Andy Sipowicz)*, Gordon Clapp
(Det Greg Medavoy), Bill Brochtrup *(John Irvin)*, James McDaniel
(Lt. Arthur Fancy), Jimmy Smits *(Det Bobby Simone)*,
Rick Schroder *(Det Danny Sorenson)*
Writers: Steven Bochco & David Milch
Producers: Steven Bochco, Mark Tinker & Steven DePaul
First Broadcast (US): 21 September 1993 – 1 March 2005
Runtime: 261 episodes x 45 min
DVD: 20th Century Fox 2003

To me, *NYPD Blue* is the direct descendant of *Hill Street Blues**. But in fact its pedigree goes right back to shows like *Naked City**. Set in Manhattan's 15th Precinct, it shows the stresses and strains on the cops' lives as well as the crimes they have to solve. First main man was David Caruso as Detective John Kelly, who soon quit, heading for the richer pastures of Hollywood which turned out to be not quite as rich as he expected. But he soon recovered and now stars in *CSI:Miami**. Actually I enjoyed the films he made, but that's for another book. Caruso's lead role was inherited by Jimmy Smits as Detective Bobby Simone. (Smits almost got the part of Don Johnson's sidekick in *Miami Vice**. Not many people know that.) But he left too and Rick Schroder took lead mantle, playing Detective Danny Sorenson. But the backbone of the series was always Dennis Franz as Detective Andy Sipowicz. Fat, grumpy, alcoholic, Andy just kept on keeping on, becoming, despite his bad habits, the character I loved most in the series and winning award after award as he went.

weblinks

www.imdb.com/title/tt0106079/
www.imdb.com/media/rm4203846144/tt0106079?slideshow=1
www.youtube.com/watch?v=mF5BFTCWzTg&feature=related
en.wikipedia.org/wiki/NYPD_Blue
www.tv.com/nypd-blue/show/219/summary.html
www.amazon.co.uk/NYPD-Blue-One-Dennis-Franz/dp/B00008WQ8O/

5. THE BILL

UK – ITV (Twenty Six Seasons)
Cast: Graham Cole *(PC Tony Stamp)*, Simon Rouse *(DCI Jack Meadows)*,
Trudie Goodwin *(Sgt June Ackland)*, Jeff Stewart *(PC Reg Hollis)*,
Mark Wingett *(DC Carver)*, Eric Richard *(Sgt Bob Cryer)*,
John Salthouse *(Det Insp Galloway)*
Writer: Geoff McQueen
Producers: Johnathan Young, Paul Marquess, James Hall & Tim Key
First Broadcast (UK):16 October 1984 – Present
Runtime: 2398+ episodes x 30 min & 60 min
DVD: Network 2007

Racists, murderers, adulterers, alcoholics, kidnappers, arsonists, bombers, liars, thieves, and that's just the coppers, and not even the really bent ones, who roam the streets of Sun Hill, surely the oddest nick in the Metropolitan Police area, as it seems to encompass not only Canary Wharf and the City, but also both banks of the Thames, as well as Soho, Tooting, Clapham, Croydon Market, and the leafy lanes of suburbia. From the most luxurious penthouses and town houses, to the skankiest estates and squats in London, though the map on the CID office wall shows Hackney and the Isle of Dogs. But never mind. *The Bill* sat astride the capital city like a colossus of crime busting boys in blue and plain clothes. I thought it always would, but in March this year, the dreadful news arrived that it was to be axed at the end of the year, and the rumour was that Sun Hill police station would be blown to hell and gone. Boo hoo! The final episode went out at the end of August this year, and the building did survive.

First seen as an episode of *Storyboard* called *Woodentops* in August 1983, it has run ever since with only short breaks. The cast has come and gone over the years, and has featured more stars in the making than can be listed here. Strange things happen though. A lot of the cops who turn up all keen and fresh faced, have earlier been seen as villains, and several actors have appeared in myriad supporting roles. And then some characters just disappear (one, it is rumoured, went out to fetch a pencil and never returned). But the worst case of writing a character out was the case of Jeff Stewart who played Reg Hollis for many years, and bore the brunt of his colleagues' sarcasm and contempt, but in fact was probably the best policeman of the lot, who was sacked from the cast, and ended up in hospital, and the only reference to his leaving was one line spoken by Inspector Gina Gold (Roberta Taylor). Shame on them!

I recently watched the first three series on DVD, and what a difference twenty-seven years has made. In those dim and distant days, the WPCs carried shoulder bags, and wore skirts and black stockings. It was even rumoured there was suspender belt action. (Did I mention sexist, by the way?) Interviews were done in offices without legal presence, and PACE (The Police and Criminal Evidence Act) was described by one custody sergeant as 'a pain in the arse.' And the language they used to each other. 'Piss off' was the favourite greeting in the canteen. 'Don't stand there like a prick' from sergeant to new recruit. Would they put that in the script now? Not a chance. And maybe that's one of the reasons that the ratings have fallen.

In the beginning the stars of the show were Detective Inspector Roy Galloway, played in the pilot by Robert Pugh, but replaced in the actual first series by the marvellous John Salthouse. Salthouse played him as the grouchiest, most bad tempered copper ever. He always acted like he could start a fight in an empty office, and often did. Galloway's nemesis in the station originally was Sergeant Wilding, played by Peter Dean, who went off to become an *EastEnder*, and Eric Richard took over as Sergeant Cryer, and lasted for years, before being pensioned off. Salthouse and Cryer were the dream team. Always bitching at each other like an old married couple, but always ready to support one another against the bosses.

The other long serving character from the start was June Ackland (Trudie Goodwin) aka St June, who was introduced in episode one, and almost made the final cut, but not quite. I was amazed to see her smoking in those early episodes, and she was missing a tooth. Blimey! But it wasn't long before she went for some expensive orthodontry, and all her pearlies were present and correct.

Another classic character was Detective Inspector Burnside (previously Detective Sergeant Burnside, bent as a nine bob note) played by Chris Eccleston, who went on to star in one of the show's spinoff series, simply called *Burnside*. The other spinoffs were *Beech on the Run*, *Beech Is Back* starring Billy Murray as yet another bent Sun Hill detective, and *MIT Murder Investigation*

Team. Interestingly enough, Billy Murray was last seen advertising one of those 'no win – no fee' lawyer firms on satellite TV. Make of that what you will.

After years of two-hour long episodes being broadcast per week at 8pm, football knocked the Wednesday episode into touch, then, in an attempt to confront more adult issues, it was switched to 9pm on a Thursday. But as I explained, not for much longer. However, for the housebound, unemployed and me, old episodes are repeated daily on a couple of satellite channels. So, on any given day with the aid of a DVD recorder (or video recorder if you're me) it's possible to watch four or five different series, and see the cast age and grow younger in front of your eyes. (Since I wrote that I've entered the 21st century and got a Sky+ box. Who would ever have thought it?)

There were two things the Sun Hill boys always did wrong. If they spotted a suspect, they always shouted for him or her to stand still, which of course they never did, allowing a chase to be filmed, usually through a council estate, and usually at first the suspect escaped. Secondly, when on 'obbo', the cops always sat right in front of wherever they were observing, and never did the villains notice. And they should learn never to buy a cup of coffee whilst out on patrol, as inevitably, a call would come through and the coffee end up in a bin.

When the show ends it will certainly be missed on the Isle of Dogs where I live, where a lot of filming takes place, as you could often get a cup of tea and a bacon sandwich from the catering van if you looked like an extra from the show, which believe me a lot of inhabitants of the Island do. Also, we'll miss the faux coppers and police cars you'd see about, considering we hardly ever see a real one.

Early episodes are available on DVD through Network as I said, but they're expensive with no subtitles, as the audio track is a bit dodgy to say the least.

weblinks

www.imdb.com/title/tt0084987/
www.youtube.com/watch?v=RBKHdFphgQk
en.wikipedia.org/wiki/The_bill
www.tv.com/the-bill/show/1023/summary.html
www.thebill.com/
www.amazon.co.uk/Bill-1-3-Complete-DVD/dp/B000WDVMQQ/

4. HAZELL

UK – ITV (Two Seasons)
Cast: Nicholas Ball *(James Hazell)*, Roddy McMillan *('Choc' Minty)*,
Desmond McNamara *(Cousin Tel)*, Peter Bourke *(Graham Morris)*
Writer: PB Yuill
Producers: Tim Aspinall, Juliet Grimm & June Roberts
First Broadcast (UK): 16 January 1978 – 5 July 1979
Runtime: 22 episodes x 60 min
DVD: Network 2004

This was originally written for *British Crime Writing: An Encyclopaedia*, edited by Barry Forshaw and published by Greenwood World Publishing of Westport Connecticut, under the name of Brian Ritterspak, but in fact the truth can now be told that it was I. (And I didn't choose that silly name.) With the kind permission of all concerned I'm allowed to reprint it here. Thanks.

'Down these mean streets a man must go' is Raymond Chandler's famous quote about his hero, private detective Philip Marlowe. But it might just as well apply to James 'Jimmy' Hazell. But in his case the streets are not in Los Angeles but dear old London town. Adapted from the novels by Gordon Williams and Terry Venables (yes, that one) under the pseudonym PB Yuill, Thames Television made twenty-two one hour (less advertisement breaks) episodes between 1978 and 1980 starring Nicholas Ball as Hazell, Roddy McMillan as 'Choc' Minty his policeman nemesis, and Desmond McNamara as his ever present accomplice Cousin Tel, plus the usual cast of character actors who seemed to pop up in every drama series of the times, including *The Sweeney**, whose time slot *Hazell* filled admirably. Overseen by Verity Lambert, head of drama at Thames, and a mover and shaker of the period, and written by some of the great dramatists who worked in popular drama then, like Tony Hoare and Trevor Preston, great things were expected of the series, which never seemed to realise its full potential although, now, the episodes have a wonderful, quirky take on the days before mobile phones, the internet and global warming.

Invalided out of the Met due to a dodgy ankle, and recently divorced because of a love of the bottle, Hazell sets up shop in a seedy office where he offers his services as a private eye cockney style. Complete with deadpan voiceovers, Ball was magnificent as the weary loser shadowed by Minty who often used him as a patsy when officialdom was thwarted, their constant bickering just like a marriage of opposites who stayed together more out of habit than love, although the detective's use of a Triumph Stag as a vehicle in which to work undercover often meant Cousin Tel appropriating a more nondescript vehicle, and sadly the locations of London were few and far between, most of the series being studio bound.

Violent for the times, *Hazell* was cancelled early. The first series is available on DVD through Network/Thames/Fremantle Media, although the sudden jumps from tape to film and back again can be disconcerting. The second series, although advertised, has never appeared.

Crime writer Mark Timlin is quoted as saying: 'Without *Hazell* there would have been no Sharman', and in fact on closer examination the comparison seems more like daylight robbery than homage. But as another famous man said: 'Talent borrows, genius steals' even though to describe Timlin as a genius seems to be going a bit far, although he would probably disagree. But compare the books and their relative TV series and you'll probably get my drift.

Ball never seemed to hit the top spot in his career that many felt he deserved, and there were rumours of a troubled private life, but he still pops up from time to time on TV, rather more rotund than in the days of *Hazell,* but always worth a look.

That was the original, and I'm still searching for the second series DVD. Ball in fact lived for a time just round the corner from me in Kennington, with his then wife Pamela Stephenson, opposite a smashing little pub (until they modernised, and ruined it) whose name escapes me. Nicholas, it seemed, spent too long at the bar, and was once seen being pursued by Pamela, frying pan in hand. I never saw the incident, and it might just be jolly South London hyperbole.

weblinks

www.imdb.com/title/tt0077020/
www.youtube.com/watch?v=KR-jU0NpjE0
en.wikipedia.org/wiki/Hazell_(TV_series)
www.tv.com/hazell/show/10021/summary.html
www.amazon.co.uk/Hazell-Complete-First-Nicholas-Ball/dp/B00018HU0E/

3. MINDER

UK – ITV (Ten Seasons)
Cast: George Cole *(Arthur Daley)*, Glynn Edwards *(Dave Harris)*,
Dennis Waterman *(Terry McCann)*, Gary Webster *(Ray Daley)*,
Patrick Malahide *(Det Sgt Albert 'Charlie' Chisholm)*, Michael Povey
(DC 'Taff' Jones), Peter Childs *(Det Sgt Ronald 'Kenny' Rycott)*
Writers: Leon Griffiths & Tony Hoare
Producers: Ian Toynton, George Taylor & Lloyd Shirley
First Broadcast (UK): 29 October 1979 – 10 March 1994
Runtime: 106 episodes x 60 min & 2 episodes x 90 min
DVD: Clear Vision Video 2007

What can I say about *Minder* that hasn't already been said? Like *Miami Vice**,
it changed the world. Or at least the UK, where nice, well-behaved middle
class children (and adults too) started talking like they'd been dragged up
in Shepherd's Bush or Bethnal Green. But it was a flop on its debut, and only
saved by the skin of its teeth.

Arthur Daley, a bravura performance by George Cole, was a ducker and diver
of the first water. Running a used car lot round the back of Fulham (I think
it was Fulham, although in many people's eyes, it was South London based)
and a lock up full of dodgy gear. He employs Terry McCann, an ex-con with
the brain of a Muppet, a back as strong as a mule, and a heart as big as a
house. An ex-boxer, he can throw a righteous left hook and Arthur makes
sure that he never gets his just reward for the jobs he finds him. Terry looks
after pubs, clubs, dance halls, villains of every stripe, and always comes out
second best to Arthur's Artful Dodgery way. But, there is also a wonderful
father son vibe, and they drink together down at the Winchester club under
the watchful eye of Dave, the owner/barman, who constantly tries to get
Arthur to pay his bar tab, as Arthur and Terry try to avoid their collars being
felt by their twin nemesises (nemisisi?) DS Chisholm and Sergeant Rycott,
(Patrick Malahide and Peter Childs. Strangely, if you put Malahide into my
spell checker, it comes out as 'baldie', which he was), assisted by the thickest

copper, DC Jones (Michael Povey), in history who never quite manage to bring either to justice.

Most London actors have made appearances including George Layton, and a frighteningly young Ray Winstone. Dennis Waterman co-wrote the theme tune *I Could Be So Good For You*, with Gerard Kenny and sang it over the credits. That was the Christmas hit mentioned in my introduction, and even *Arthur Daley (E's Alright)* by The Firm made the UK Top 20 in 1982.

It's constantly repeated on satellite and all the series are available on Clear Vision Video.

Then, in 1991, Waterman left and Gary Webster came in as Arthur's nephew. Always skint, but changed suits about ten times every episode. Avoid. But not as enthusiastically as the diabolical remake made a couple of years ago, with Shane Richie as Arthur's other nephew, (I think) I lasted ten minutes into the first episode and binned it.

weblinks

www.imdb.com/title/tt0078657/
www.youtube.com/watch?v=ylKK-iB_mZI
en.wikipedia.org/wiki/Minder_(TV_series)
www.tv.com/minder-1979/show/2122/summary.html
www.amazon.co.uk/Minder-1-DVD/dp/B000MZGVEW/

2. HOMICIDE: LIFE ON THE STREET

USA – CH4 (Seven Seasons)
Cast: Richard Belzer *(Det John Munch)*, Clark Johnson *(Det Meldrick Lewis)*, Yaphet Kotto *(Lt. Al Giardello)*, Kyle Secor *(Det Tim Bayliss)*, Andre Braugher *(Det Frank Pembleton)*
Writers: Paul Attanasio & David Simon
Producers: Jim Finnerty, Tom Fontana, Barry Levinson & Gail Mutrux
First Broadcast (US): 31 January 1993 – 21 May 1999
Runtime: 122 episodes x 60 min
DVD: Freemantle Home Entertainment 2010

Without doubt one of the great cop shows ever made. *Homicide*, as it is simply known round my house, ran for six years in the Nineteen Nineties. Set partly in the Homicide Division Office of the Baltimore, Maryland police force itself, and partly on the streets of the city, there is very little glamour about the motley crew looking for justice as the murders pile up, and are religiously listed on a white board that takes up one wall. Red for live, black for solved.

The series was based on the best selling book, *Homicide: A Year on the Killing Streets* by Baltimore journalist David Simon, who later created *The Wire**.

weblinks

www.imdb.com/title/tt0106028/
www.imdb.com/video/screenplay/vi1722614041/
en.wikipedia.org/wiki/Homicide:_Life_on_the_Street
www.tv.com/homicide-life-on-the-street/show/110/summary.html
www.amazon.co.uk/Homicide-Life-Street-Complete-Collection/dp/B003110MR6/

SO, HERE IT IS.
WHAT YOU'VE ALL BEEN WAITING FOR.
OR AT LEAST I HOPE YOU'VE GOT THIS FAR.

TOP OF THE POPS.
WHAT ELSE COULD IT BE BUT...?

1.   THE SWEENEY

UK – ITV (Four Seasons)
Cast: John Thaw *(Det Insp Jack Regan)*, Dennis Waterman *(Det Sgt George Carter)*, Tony Allen *(Bill the Driver)*, Garfield Morgan *(Det Chief Insp Frank Haskins)*
Writers: Ian Kennedy Martin & Trevor Preston
Producers: Ted Childs, Mary Morgan, Lloyd Shirley & George Taylor
First Broadcast (UK): 2 January 1975 – 28 December 1978
Runtime: 53 episodes x 60 min
DVD: Network 2007

In 2002, shortly after John Thaw died, I wrote this piece for *Crime Time* magazine under the title *Don't Look Back in a Granada*. It's reprinted here verbatim. Just don't forget it was eight years ago, and tastes change, including mine. Still the best TV crime show ever though.

Da-da. Da-da. Da-de-da-da-da-da-da-da-dah-Dah

Oh what bliss it was to be alive when Thames TV first broadcast that clarion call to cop-show fans everywhere.

It introduced the first episode of *The Sweeney* on 2nd January 1975 with an episode called *Ringer* starring Brian Blessed, coincidentally one of the early stars of *Z-Cars**, which itself was dying a death on BBC1 at the same time. What a start to a new year! And what a start to the best TV police procedural ever, although if that was police procedure in the seventies then God save us all. But of course half the fun was that it wasn't authentic, at least we didn't think it was. Later revelations showed us that maybe it was closer to the truth than we ever imagined, which might indicate why we're in the mess we're in now.

At the time, it seemed that *The Sweeney* was going to change British TV cop shows for ever. And it almost did. It teetered on the edge, but in the end it all came back to *Midsomer Murders**, as in our hearts we knew it would. Nothing that good could ever last.

But for a few glorious years...

But that wasn't the first we'd seen of that particular section of the thin blue line. *Regan* was a one-off eighty minute film in the *Armchair Cinema* strand shown on the 4th June 1974 at 8.30 pm. John Thaw played Detective-Inspector Jack Regan. The most rambunctious, boozing, birding, thin-line walking copper since...

Well, there never was one. Not in the UK anyway.

The show had an audience of over seven million and, on the strength of it, another thirteen episodes were commissioned to be called *The Sweeney* after the Cockney rhyming slang Sweeney Todd – Flying Squad. All in all Euston films made a further fifty-three episodes, the final one being aired over the Christmas holidays in 1978. So historically *The Sweeney* embraced Glam Rock, Punk, *Star Wars*, The Queen's Silver Jubilee and the death of the old Labour party.

Most of the characters from *Regan* were reprised in the series, including George Carter, Regan's ever loyal skipper (Detective-Sergeant). Carter was played by Dennis Waterman. The two actors fitted together on screen like fish and chips, Scotch and Coke, cheese on toast. They just worked, and every bloke wanted a mate like they were mates. One who was ready to pile in, no questions asked, watch your back, and lie in their teeth to get you out of bother.

So what else was important about *The Sweeney*?

Well, you've got to remember that, as it was being shown, so was *Dixon of Dock Green*. Yeah, it's hard to imagine, but old George was walking the same mean streets of London as Regan and Carter right up until 1976. Doesn't bear thinking about, does it?

So apart from anything else, it blew shows like that old chestnut right out of the water, born as it was out of *Public Eye**, *Callan** and *Special Branch**. And allowed others like *Gangsters* and *Target* to be made. And it was all on film, not like so many other shows at the time with bits of film interspersed with video. Just like the writers wanted it to be. Writers like Ian and Troy Kennedy Martin, Trevor Preston and Tony Hoare amongst others. And what writing. Not for them the clumsy caution that the actors in *The Bill**

and other police shows have to use now. Just 'Get your trousers on, you're nicked,' and back to the station for a well-earned Scotch from the bottle hidden in the bottom desk drawer.

That old scotch bottle was one of the many props that were as important in their way as the stars and the script.

First, the clothes. Flares. Massive, elephant-sized flares over clumpy, high-heeled, platform-soled boots with zips up the sides. And jackets with Concorde-sized lapels, kipper ties, long shirt collars, either penny round or pointed. But no button-down or tabs. That was ten years ago mod, and wouldn't come back into fashion for ten more. The shirts were form fitting then, with sleeves so narrow that they cut the skin on the inside of your elbows, and viciously, button-poppingly pleated at the back no matter how big a gut they exposed. And watching *The Sweeney* now, it seems that not many actors had a gym regime in those days. And there was a lot of suede about, but we don't talk about that.

You may laugh now, but at the time these guys were at the cutting edge of fashion, the epitome of cool and young men all over the country wanted to emulate them, and some of us did. I did, and made a bloody fool of myself more than once.

Then there were the motors. Never cars – always motors, or occasionally wheels. The plain clothes drove Fords. Consuls, Granadas, and Coke bottle Cortinas. The uniforms, or woodentops as Regan described them, had Mk 1 Escorts and Rovers mostly, with the odd Allegro thrown in to make our mouths water. The villains drove anything from flash Yanks in all colours of the rainbow, Rollers, Triumph Stags, Range Rovers. Almost anything expensive. But of course their favourites, and the favourites to be wrecked in some puddle jumping, fence wrecking chase through the wilds of the then still derelict Docklands, were beautiful S-Type Jaguars. No wonder they're so expensive now, as the property masters must've bought job lots of them cheap, and wrecked them wholesale. Nobody wanted them then; once again it would be ten years before they came back into fashion as yuppie classics.

And guns.

Blimey, they handed them out like sweets in those days. The cops used short-barrelled revolvers, and the bad guys... Well, take your pick. Machine guns, semi-automatic. Anything that would shoot in fact, and shoot them they did. The armourer must've spent a fortune on blank ammunition.

As much props as the above were the birds.

Lynda Bellingham (the OXO mum) as a dolly bird. Lynda La Plante (award winning TV writer and producer) as a dolly bird. Geraldine James (*Band of Gold*) as a dolly bird. Lesley-Anne Down (*Upstairs, Downstairs*) as a dolly bird. And loads of other actresses who now have a few years and more dignity on them, whose faces you know, but names you wouldn't recognise, as dolly birds.

With the shortest mini skirts you've ever seen.

But not Ally McBeal Lycra-tight minis. More flared like the trousers, and more easily accessible as lots of boys found out around then.

And what boys they were.

Probably the most memorable were George Layton and Patrick Mower as a homo-erotic pair of heisters from Australia. They appeared in a couple of episodes, charming their way round London, and in the first actually got away from the long arm of the law.

Of course, much of the fun now is spotting future stars, and there were plenty of them to spot. Including what looks like half the cast of the early *EastEnders*, most of *Only Fools and Horses*, and even refugees from *Crossroads*. It was a British luvvie fest. John Hurt, Ian Hendry, Warren Mitchell, Warren Clarke, Bill Maynard, Michael Elphick, Maurice Roëves, and dozens more shrugged on donkey jackets and Doc Martens, and foolishly took on Regan and Carter, only to end up dead, or eating Her Majesty's porridge.

And never forget Harry South's music.

The main theme for the opening credits to which little kids would soon be heard singing 'Swee-nee, swee-nee', and the wonderfully mournful end credit music.

Time's verdict on the show can be harsh. It's accused of being, amongst other things, sexist, homophobic and racist. And it almost certainly was, at least by new Millennium standards. Things were different all those years ago, and although we appear to have defeated this trio of prejudices, is life any better for minorities now than it was then? I somehow doubt it. It just appears that way to the chattering classes so they can sleep safer in their beds. Overly violent was another charge. And it's true it was. Never have punches been so amplified, and never have baseball bats been wielded with such enthusiasm. I've even heard a rumour that Channel 5 censored some scenes when they repeated the show. It seems strange in this so called free society of ours that nanny always knows best. They used to try to change history by burning books. Now they chop up old TV series.

But let's not get too serious. At the core of *The Sweeney* was always a big element of comedy.

Hence Ronnie Fraser as Titus Oates in Series 3, Diana Dors as the terrifying Mrs Rix in Series 4, and Morecambe and Wise, in the final episode ever made. Though not the last one shown, which in fact was a sad epitaph for what had been the toughest show on British TV.

There were also two films made for the cinema, but in my opinion, the less said about them the better.

To some of us it will always be the seventies, and we'll look back with fondness to a low-rise London, Take-6 suits, Blue Nun, Capri Ghias, and of course *The Sweeney*.

I miss it. I think I'm going to go home and dig out a Sweeney video.

For more *Sweeney* related information, check out: *Fags, Slags, Blags & Jags* – Mike Kenwood & George Williams – Uslag Press – £9.99

Shutit! A Fan's Guide to 70s Cops on the Box – Martin Day & Keith Topping – Virgin Books – £6.99. And the show still turns up on satellite from time to time. Check out your listings magazine. That was then, and this is now. The complete series. 53 episodes, not 52 as is usually reported. The final series had 14 episodes, not the usual 13 (presumably so that Thaw could bow out gracefully. In a black cab of course. How *EastEnders* of him) and are available on DVD from Network, complete with the two features. There's another book also. *Sweeney! The Official Companion* by Robert Fairclough & Mike Kenwood (Reynolds & Hearn – £14.99), though I suspect all three might be out of print. Strange how the authors all come in pairs. That might be because it was so much fun to sit down with a mate, some beer and snacks and get into the shows. There's probably more, but I don't have them. Merchandise was plentiful too at the time. Novels, T-shirts, a board game, and several annuals. I'd be in the market for any of those too.

weblinks

www.imdb.com/title/tt0071059/
www.youtube.com/watch?v=D99O6oTJVHo
en.wikipedia.org/wiki/The_Sweeney
www.tv.com/the-sweeney/show/5242/summary.html
www.amazon.co.uk/Sweeney-Complete-Box-Set-DVD/dp/B000XYFGIE/

There you have it, the hot hundred TV crime series in the opinion of this writer. The good, the bad and the ugly as it were. But even the bad can seem good in retrospect and bring back pleasant memories, so that's why I included a few. So where's the elusive other one? I hear you ask, or at least I hope you do. Number one-hundred-and-one. Well now, there can only be one can't there.

Sharman, the series. An event that changed my life forever. But I don't want to write about it myself. Too close you see. So instead, let's go back to the inestimable and absolutely essential, for any crime fan (but you'll need deep pockets), *British Crime Writing: An Encyclopedia*, where Ali Karim wrote a piece on the series. With thanks to him, Barry Forshaw who edited the two volumes, and Greenwood World Publishing who published them, and kind permission from all, here it is. . .

101. SHARMAN (TV series)

UK – ITV
THE TURNAROUND [PILOT]
Cast: Clive Owen *(Nick Sharman)*, Bill Paterson *(James Webb)*, Rowena King *(Fiona)*, Roberta Taylor *(Aggie)*, John Salthouse *(DI Jack Robber)*
Writer: Tony Hoare
Director: Suri Krishnamma
Producers: Tony Garnett & Bill Shapter
First Broadcast (UK): 22 April 1995
Runtime: 90 min

TAKE THE A-TRAIN
Cast: Clive Owen *(Nick Sharman)*, Samantha Janus *(Jane)*, Roberta Taylor *(Aggie)*, John Salthouse *(DI Jack Robber)*, Gina Bellman *(Kiki)*
Writer: Guy Jenkin
Director: Robert Bierman
Producers: Tony Garnett & Bill Shapter
First Broadcast (UK): 4 November 1996
Runtime: 90 min

HEARTS OF STONE
Cast: Clive Owen *(Nick Sharman)*, Keith Allen *(Brady)*, Roberta Taylor *(Aggie)*, John Salthouse *(DI Jack Robber)*, Julie Graham *(Kylie)*
Writer: Paul Abbott
Director: Robert Bierman
Producers: Tony Garnett & Bill Shapter
First Broadcast (UK): 11 November 1996
Runtime: 90 min

A GOOD YEAR FOR THE ROSES
Cast: Clive Owen *(Nick Sharman)*, Ray Winstone *(George Bright)*, Adie Allen *(Dawn)*, Hugo Speer *(Mayles)*, Collette Brown *(Tracey)*, John Salthouse *(DI Jack Robber)*, Roberta Taylor *(Aggie)*
Writer: Dusty Hughes
Director: Matthew Evans
Producers: Tony Garnett & Bill Shapter
First Broadcast (UK): 18 November 1996
Runtime: 90 min

SHARMAN [EPISODE FOUR]

Cast: Clive Owen *(Nick Sharman)*, Anton Lesser *(Galilee)*, Adie Allen *(Dawn)*, Emma Cunningham *(Carol)*, Collette Brown *(Tracey)*, Danny Webb *(Durban)*, John Salthouse *(DI Jack Robber)*, Roberta Taylor *(Aggie)*
Writer: Mick Ford
Director: Matthew Evans
Producers: Tony Garnett & Bill Shapter
First Broadcast (UK): 25 November 1996
Runtime: 90 min
DVD: Sharman – The Complete Series – Network 2010

Actor Clive Owen was coming into prominence in the mid 1990s, following his appearance in the TV series *Chancer*; when he was cast as the tough South-London PI Nick Sharman [World Productions for Carlton/ITV] based on the gritty novels by Mark Timlin. As a character, Sharman has his share of problems: a former police officer whose career was derailed due to drink and drugs which also cost him his marriage; he lives on the edge as a private eye scratching a living in the alleyways of South London. He has a daughter, Judith, to support as well as a string of girlfriends and low-lifes who are forever on his case. The young Clive Owen is perfectly cast as Sharman, as he has the bad-boy good looks and a sneer that breathes life into his portrayal of Sharman but, most importantly, his eyes show the pain and the void in his heart brought about from his hard life, living day-to-day and from woman to woman.

The first of the Nick Sharman adventures was the feature-length *The Turnaround* [1995] based on the book of the same name, and adapted by writer Tony Hoare and directed by Suri Krishnamma. *The Turnaround* actually follows the novel's plot closely. Sharman is on a hunt to clear his name, following a case in which he's hired by a James Webb [Bill Paterson] to find the men who murdered his sister and her family. The case goes seriously off the rails and Sharman is on a race to clear his name as he becomes the principal suspect to the murders. Timlin makes a cameo appearance but blink and you'll miss him. This episode pilot for the Sharman series attracted 10 million viewers and was the only episode released on VHS.

It was not until 1996 that we'd see Owen return as Sharman in *Take the A-Train* [Episode 1] with supporting actress Samantha Janus playing a Page 3 model. This time, Sharman investigates the [apparent] suicide of a former police colleague who appears to have thrown himself off a tower-block. Sharman's investigation gets involved in a gang war in the neon world of club land. *Hearts of Stone* [Episode 2] is probably the best of the series, due to writer Paul Abbott following the novel's story closely. Sharman is in pursuit of a couple of heavy-handed debt collectors when he gets roped by former colleagues from the police drugs-squad to infiltrate a dope smuggling operation. It is a mission he can't refuse as the alternative offered is fifteen years on the wrong side of prison bars. The episode features a manic Keith Allen playing to form. *A Good Year for the Roses* [Episode 3] is actually based on Nick Sharman's debut in print, and features a strong performance from Ray Winstone. Sharman is hired as a minder for a lesbian dancing duo when Winstone (playing hard man George Bright) hires Sharman to track down his missing eighteen-year-old daughter. The case takes a turn for the worse when Sharman finds Bright's daughter dead, overdosed in a squalid squat. *Sharman* [Episode 4], the last in the series, was an original screenplay but does feature a scene from Timlin's novel *Pretend We're Dead* and would be the last in this cult series.

Apparently due to the uproar about violence on TV, in the aftermath of the Dunblane shootings, Carlton / ITV cancelled Sharman, just as the series was finding its feet. Tragically it has never been repeated on terrestrial or satellite TV, and is long overdue for a DVD release. In this final episode we see Sharman roped into a case of money laundering and dodgy dealings at a local bank. Simultaneously, he's about to get married. Although Nick Sharman is British, his roots from Timlin's novels are pure Raymond Chandler as the cynical eye he deploys comes from the American PI tradition. Timlin will forever be remembered for Nick Sharman, as Chandler is always associated with Philip Marlowe, and those with long memories will always associate Clive Owen with Nick Sharman, despite whatever he does under the shadow of Hollywood's famous hills.

weblinks

Mark Timlin – Website: www.nicksharman.co.uk
ThrillerUK – Nick Sharman Special www.thrilleruk.fsnet.co.uk/latest.htm
CrimeTime – Rise and Fall of Nick Sharman
www.crimetime.co.uk/features/marktimlin.php
Fantastic Fiction www.fantasticfiction.co.uk/t/mark-timlin/
Thrilling Detective www.thrillingdetective.com/sharman.html
No Exit Press www.noexit.co.uk/authorpages/mark_timlin.php

Couldn't have put it better myself, and although the end is nigh, there's still a few bits more to enjoy, as there were more series than I was contracted to write about, so what follows are the outtakes. But interesting nevertheless, plus one dog. Please read on.

OUTTAKES

TRAFFIK

UK – CH4 (One Season)
Cast: Bill Paterson *(Jack Lithgow)*, Lindsay Duncan *(Helen Rosshalde)*,
Fritz Muller-Scherz *(Ulli)*, Jamal Shah *(Fazal)*, Talet Hussain *(Tariq Butt)*,
Vincenzo Benestante *(Domenquez)*, George Kukura *(Karl Rosshalde)*,
Ismat hah Jahan *(Sabira)*, Raahi Raza *(Khushal)* Roohi Raza *(Naseem)*
Writer: Simon Moore
Producers: Christabel Albery & Brian Eastman
First Broadcast (UK): 22 June 1989 – 24 July 1989
Runtime: 6 Episodes x 60 min

DVD: Cinema Club 2003

One of the best of the rest, starring the wonderful Bill Paterson as Jack Lithgow, – a crusading politician trying to halt the opium trade from the North-West Frontier Province of Pakistan. The location moves from there to the UK and Germany, showing the many people involved in drug trafficking, and the repercussions of the business, from a poor farmer to a wealthy drugs baron. Later made into a 2000 big screen movie starring Michael Douglas and Catherine Zeta-Jones, that for once wasn't a piece of rubbish.

weblinks

www.imdb.com/title/tt0096716/
www.youtube.com/show/traffik?pl=09538590488F2B39
en.wikipedia.org/wiki/Traffik
www.amazon.co.uk/Traffik-DVD-Bill-Paterson/dp/B00005KCAR

RED CAP

UK – ITV (Two Seasons)
Cast: John Thaw *(Sergeant John Mann)*
Writers: Troy Kennedy-Martin & Julian Bond
Producer: John Bryce
First Broadcast (UK): 17 October 1964 – June 25 1966
Runtime: 26 episodes x 60 min in Black and White
DVD: Network 2005

The late John Thaw appeared as Sergeant John Mann, officer of Her Majesty's Royal Military Police Special Investigation Branch, in his first starring role in a TV series. Amazingly, he was only twenty-two when filming began, but did look older. This one is a brilliant prologue to Thaw's tough guy appearances, particularly in *The Sweeney**, which tragically ended with him playing Inspector bloody Morse and listening to opera. As you might guess, neither *Morse* nor its dull sequel *Lewis* is featured in this book.

Redcap was a great success at the time and ran for two series, and the supporting cast list reads like a dream, and included Diana Rigg, Keith Barron, Windsor Davies, Alan Lake and Garfield Morgan, later of course to turn up as Thaw's harassed boss in *The Sweeney**.

There was even a *Red Cap* annual published for Christmas, and if anyone's got one I'm in the market for it.

By the way, not to be confused with *RedCap* with Tamzin Outhwaite playing a maverick military police woman (yawn).

weblinks

www.imdb.com/title/tt0058843/
www.youtube.com/watch?v=7m1fqbnOqBo
www.tv.com/redcap-1964/show/20475/summary.html
en.wikipedia.org/wiki/Redcap_(TV_series)
www.amazon.co.uk/Redcap-Complete-First-John-Thaw/dp/B0009F68FC/

SPOOKS

UK – BBC1 (Nine Seasons)

Cast: Peter Firth *(Harry Pearce)*, Hugh Simon *(Malcolm Wynn-Jones)*, Nicola Walker *(Ruth Evershed)*, Rupert Penry-Jones *(Adam Carter)*, Miranda Raison *(Jo Portman)*, Hermione Norris *(Ros Myers)*

Writer: David Wolstencroft

Producers: Simon Crawford-Collins, Jane Featherstone & Andrew Woodhead

First Broadcast (UK): 13 May 2002 – Present

Runtime: 80 episodes x 60 min

DVD: E1 Entertainment 2003

Once again, not strictly speaking a cop show, but certainly one I watch time and time again, so hard luck.

Spooks are spies working for MI5, foiling terrorists by any means possible. And that includes black ops, wet work and torture. What fun it must be, being able to do anything you feel like and get paid; and get laid, as the spooks do quite often in this long-running series.

It all started at the beginning of the new century with Matthew Macfadyen as Tom Quinn and the rest of the Section D team at MI5 HQ in London, headed by Harry Pearce (Peter Firth). Members of the team come and go, as the producers are quite sadistic, killing off the cast in violent ways, one of the best featuring a deep fat fryer and a fillet of face. Not battered, but pretty well done to a turn.

The ninth series is running as I write.

weblinks

www.imdb.com/title/tt0160904/
en.wikipedia.org/wiki/Spooks
www.tv.com/spooks/show/10812/summary.html
www.youtube.com/watch
www.amazon.co.uk/Spooks-Complete-BBC-1-DVD/dp/

THE BEIDERBECKE TRILOGY:
THE BEIDERBECKE AFFAIR / TAPES / CONNECTION

UK – ITV (Three Seasons)
Cast: James Bolam *(Trevor Chaplin)*, Barbara Flynn *(Jill Swunburne)*,
Terence Rigby *(Big Al)*, Dominic Jephcott *(Det Sgt Hobson)*,
Dudley Sutton *(Mr Carter)*, Keith Smith *(Mr Wheeler)*, Malcolm Storry
(Mr Peterson), Beryl Reid *(Sylvia)*, Danny Schiller *(Little Norm)*, Darren
Bennet *(Gary)*, Gaynor Kitchen *(Sharon)*, Dave Leslie *(Man Opposite)*, Sean
Scanlan *(DC Joe)*, Patrick Drury *(Ivan)*, George Costigan *(DC Ben)*
Writer: Alan Plater
Producers: David Cunliffe & Anne W. Gibbons
First Broadcast (UK): 6 January 1985 – 18 December 1988
Runtime: 12 Episodes x 60 min
DVD:Network 2007

Another winner, or rather, three winners for James Bolam. Pussy-whipped woodwork teacher Trevor Chaplin, played by our hero, and his overbearing girlfriend, English teacher Jill Swinburne (Barbara Flynn) work together at a Leeds comprehensive school. Chaplin is a jazz fan, and she wants to be elected to the council. Chaplin seeks a set of Bix Beiderbecke LPs. Remember them? LPs that is. Lovely stuff. But he receives something else in the mail which leads the pair into the criminal underworld where corruption flowers in those very same council chambers. They solve the mystery, and all live happily ever after. The series was a big success and returned twice more. In the second series, *Tapes*, again recorded music, or rather something recorded over recorded music, opens a can of villainous worms, but true love conquers all.

Finally, the couple get mixed up with refugees in *Connection*, and that was all they wrote. Possibly just as well, as there's only so much Beiderbecke music one can bear. (In the series it was replicated by Kenny Baker.)

Affair: www.imdb.com/title/tt0086668/
Tapes: www.imdb.com/title/tt0092629/
Connection: www.imdb.com/title/tt0094421/
en.wikipedia.org/wiki/The_Beiderbecke_Affair
en.wikipedia.org/wiki/The_Beiderbecke_Tapes
en.wikipedia.org/wiki/The_Beiderbecke_Connection
www.amazon.co.uk/Beiderbecke-Trilogy-Complete-Repackaged-DVD/dp/
www.tv.com/the-beiderbecke-affair/show/32518/summary.html

ER

USA – CH4 (Fifteen Seasons)
Cast: Noah Wyle *(Dr John Carter)*, Laura Innes *(Dr Kerry Weaver)*,
Laura Cerón *(Nurse Chuny Marquez)*, Maura Tierney *(Nurse Abby Lockhart)*,
Deezer D *(Nurse Malik Mcgrath)*, Goran Visnjic *(Dr Luka Kovac)*,
Yvette Freeman *(Nurse Haleh Adams)*, Anthony Edwards
(Dr Mark Greene), Eriq La Salle *(Dr Peter Benton)*, Emily Wagner
(Doris Pickman), Alex Kingston *(Dr Elizabeth Corday)*
Writer: Michael Crichton
Producers: Michael Crichton & John Wells
First Broadcast (US): 19 September 1994 – 2 April 2009
Runtime: 331 Episodes x 60 min 1 Episode x 90 min
DVD: Warner Home Video 2009

Now come on, I hear you say. *ER* is not a cop show. Well, if it ain't I'm a monkey's uncle. And besides I didn't spend £171 on fourteen box sets of the show not to feature it here. Let's face it, there are more cop appearances in ER than in most crime dramas. Set in the run-down Cook County Hospital in Chicago, *ER* charged across the screen for fifteen years, featuring almost unintelligible dialogue (thank God the DVDs have subtitles) and made our own *Casualty* look like local rep.

HUSTLE

UK – BBC1 (Six Seasons)
Cast: Robert Glenister *(Ash Morgan)*, Robert Vaughn *(Albert Stroller)*, Rob Jarvis *(Eddie)*, Adrian Lester *(Mickey Stone)*, Marc Warren *(Danny Blue)*, Jaime Murray *(Stacie Monroe)*, Ashley Walters *(Billy Bond)*
Writers: Tony Jordan & Bharat Nalluri
Producers: Simon Crawford Collins, Jane Featherstone & Tony Jordan
First Broadcast (UK): 24 February 2004 – Present
Runtime: 36 episodes x 60 min
DVD: Warner Home Video 2010

Actually, there are very few cops in Hustle, the how to do it show for aspiring conmen. The punters who fall for the schemes of Michael 'Mickey' Stone (Adrian Lester) and his gang usually feel too foolish to call in the law. Which is exactly how they want it.

I SPY

US – ITV (Three Seasons)
Cast: Robert Culp *(Kelly Robinson)*, Bill Cosby *(Alexander Scott)*
Writers: Morton S. Fine & David Friedkin
Producers: Morton S. Fine, David Friedkin & Sheldon Leonard
First Broadcast (US): 15 September 1965 – 15 April 1968
Runtime: 82 Episodes x 60 min
DVD: Image Entertainment 2008

Ah, those were the days it was beautiful just to be alive. The days when Bill Cosby was funny and Robert Culp was good looking. But let's not be bitchy. Let's just remember those golden hours. (Since I wrote that Robert Culp has died. Sorry mate, but the comment still stands.) *I Spy* was a slick, good looking, exciting, glossy series featuring the two heroes as spooks disguised as professional sportsmen. Culp as a tennis ace and Cosby as his trainer. In fact, in real life Culp was a professional standard player, which was handy. The duo travelled from one exotic location to another, wisecracking, chatting up glamorous women, dodging danger, and generally having a fine old time as they went. A ground-breaking series at the time in the USA, in the fact that it starred a salt and pepper team, it was still made obvious that Culp was the main man, and poor old Cosby could only romance black women. (NB. At the same time in *A Man Called Ironside*, Don Mitchell was also pushing the racial equality envelope as Mark Sanger, Ironside's major domo.) Nevertheless, it was Cosby who picked up three Emmys, before going on to become a national treasure in *The Cosby Show*. He also made a number of excellent comedy albums, but I don't know if they've stood the test of time because I sold mine. The pair later appeared together in the film *Hickey & Boggs* as two down-at-heel private eyes.

weblinks

www.imdb.com/title/tt0058816/
www.youtube.com/watch?v=WdvSD_lezvM
en.wikipedia.org/wiki/I_Spy_%281965_TV_series%29
www.tv.com/i-spy/show/571/summary.html
www.amazon.co.uk/Spy-Season-Full-Rmst-Region/dp/

KOLCHAK: THE NIGHT STALKER

US – ITV (One Season)
Cast: Darren McGavin *(Kolchak)*, Carol Lynley *(Gail Foster)*,
Simon Oakland *(Tony Vincenzo)*, Ralph Meeker *(Bernie Jenks)*
Writers: Richard Matheson & Jeffrey Grant Rice
Producer: Dan Curtis
First Broadcast (US): 13 September 1974–28 March 1975
Runtime: 20 Episodes x 60min
DVD: Universal 2006

Not to be confused with *Kojak**, Kolchak was a very different dish of tea. Played by Darren McGavin, he is a beat up, cynical, investigative reporter for the Independent News Service (INS) working out of Chicago. His speciality is killers. Vicious killers, who he tracks down as he dictates his stories into his portable tape recorder.

It all began with a pair of TV Movies, *The Night Stalker* and *The Night Strangler*, and this was horror/crime fare at its scariest. Based on a novel by Jeff Rice, *The Kolchak Papers*, it was all too much for middle America and was swiftly cancelled. What didn't help was that Rice sued the ABC Network for making the shows without his permission.

The DVD was released by Universal, so all must have been settled. What a relief!

weblinks

www.imdb.com/title/tt0067490/
www.youtube.com/watch?v=-Xfl0m6U8IE
en.wikipedia.org/wiki/Kolchak:_The_Night_Stalker
www.tv.com/kolchak-the-night-stalker/show/2694/summary.html
www.amazon.co.uk/Kolchak-Night-Stalker-Complete-DVD/dp/

THE SOPRANOS

USA – CHANNEL 4 (Six Seasons)
Cast: James Gandolfini *(Tony Soprano)*, Edie Falco *(Carmela Soprano)*,
Jamie-Lynn Sigler *(Meadow Soprano)*, Michael Imperioli
(Christopher Moltisanti), Lorraine Bracco *(Dr Jennifer Melfi)*,
Tony Sirico *(Paulie 'Walnuts' Gualtieri)*
Writer: David Chase
Producers: David Chase, Martin Bruestle, Brad Grey, Ilene S. Landress &
Henry Bronchtein
First Broadcast (US): 10 January 1999 – 10 June 2007
Runtime: 86 episodes x 60 min
DVD: Warner Home Video 2009

Another one of those shows that changed the face of TV drama, but ran out
of steam before it finished on an unsatisfying and mysterious note. Set in
New Jersey, Tony Soprano is a Mafia boss who is afraid for his mental health,
seeing a psychiatrist, but unable to tell anyone, including his wife. His HQ is
the Bada Bing club where near naked babes simulate sex with poles (lower
case), but possibly Poles (upper case) also, whilst the made men play cards
and plan villainy in the back room.

The show was a smash on both sides of the water despite (or maybe because
of) the strong language and even stronger violence.

The theme was 'Woke up this Morning' by the Alabama 3 (actually from
Brixton, South London) and even that featured gunfire.

weblinks

www.imdb.com/title/tt0141842/
www.youtube.com/watch?v=ERYpbpqxf4o
en.wikipedia.org/wiki/The_Sopranos
www.tv.com/the-sopranos/show/314/summary.html
www.amazon.co.uk/Sopranos-HBO-Complete-Seasons-Packaging/dp/

PRISON BREAK

US – SKY ONE (Four Seasons)
Cast: Dominic Purcell *(Lincoln Burrows)*, Wentworth Miller
(Michael Scofield), Amaury Nolasco *(Fernando Sucre)*,
Robert Knepper *(Theodore 'T-Bag' Bagwell)*
Writer: Paul Scheuring
Producers: Marty Adelstein, Garry A. Brown, Neal H. Moritz, Dawn
Parouse, Brett Ratner & Paul Sheuring
First Broadcast (US): 29 August 2005 – 15 May 2009
Runtime: 81 Episodes x 60 min
DVD: 20th Century Fox 2009

Lincoln Burrows (Dominic Purcell) is wrongly convicted for murder and
banged up in Fox River jail. His brother Michael Scofield (Wentworth Miller)
is determined to get him out by hook or by crook. An architect by trade, he
gets his body tattooed with the blue prints of the prison, commits a crime,
and (luckily) gets sent to the same facility. And that's when the fun begins as
he, and a pack of other prisoners, some very nasty, some stupid, some both,
especially the show's star in my opinion, Robert Knepper as Theodore 'T-Bag'
Bagwell, start to tunnel their way out. They escape, but things don't go as
planned and they all end up in a Mexican prison, where the whole escape
thing starts again.

weblinks

www.imdb.com/title/tt0455275/
en.wikipedia.org/wiki/Prison_Break
www.tv.com/prison-break/show/31635/summary.html
www.amazon.co.uk/Prison-Break-Complete-Seasons-Box/dp/

LOST

USA – SKY ONE/CH4 (Six Seasons)
Cast: Naveen Andrews *(Sayid Jarrah)*, Matthew Fox *(Jack Shephard)*,
Jorge Garcia *(Hugo 'Hurley' Reyes)*, Josh Holloway *(James 'Sawyer' Ford)*,
Daniel Dae Kim *(Jin Kwon)*, Yunjin Kim *(Sun Kwon)*,
Terry O'Quinn *(John Locke)*
Writers: JJ Abrams, Jeffrey Leiber & Damon Lindelof
Producers: JJ Abrams, Bryan Burk, Ra'uf Glasgow, Jean Higgins & Damon Lindelof
First Broadcast (US): 22 September 2004 – 23 May 2010
Runtime: 121 episodes x 42 min
DVD: Buena Vista Home Entertainment 2010

Once again, not strictly crime, but packed with bad guys, *Lost* sees an airliner crash on a Pacific island, apparently deserted but actually busier than Oxford Circus, with polar bears, scientists, ruffians, dead priests, and some kind of black smoke monster all in situ. Phew! Anyway, the survivors of the crash look to the good doctor Jack Shephard (the good shepherd – geddit. The whole show is full of quirky little details like that. Love 'em or leave 'em, I say) played by Matthew Fox, who's so handsome it hurts. He falls for Kate Austen (Evangeline Lilley) who's a woman with secrets. (In fact, everyone has secrets in the show.) In fact, she's a killer on the run, so she doesn't worry too much about going home. But they eventually do, or do they?

The show ended in 2010 with the last episode shown at the same time worldwide. Sadly it was at 5am in England and I was in the land of nod. No worries, I'll catch the DVD.

weblinks

www.imdb.com/title/tt0411008/
www.youtube.com/watch?v=5KlnQyjiZ5w&feature=related
en.wikipedia.org/wiki/Lost_%28TV_series%29
www.tv.com/lost/show/24313/summary.html
www.amazon.co.uk/Lost-Complete-Seasons-1-6-DVD/dp/

MILLENNIUM™

US (Three Seasons)
Cast: Lance Henriksen *(Frank Black)*, Terry O'Quinn *(Peter Watts)*,
Megan Gallagher *(Catherine Black)*, Brittany Tiplady *(Jordan Black)*
Writer: Chris Carter
Producers: Chris Carter, Chip Johannessen,
John Peter Kousakis, Ken Horton & Paul Rabwin
First Broadcast (US): 25 October 1996 – 21 May 1999
Runtime: 67 episodes x 45min
DVD: 20th Century Fox 2005

Here's an interesting one, starring stone-faced Lance Henriksen as serial-killer profiler Frank Black and Megan Gallagher as his long suffering wife (there's an awful lot of them in cop shows), and created by Chris Carter of *X-Files* fame.

In the first of the three series, Frank relocated his family to Seattle, after the stress of the horror he witnessed whilst working for the FBI in Washington DC. Because Frank has a unique talent. He can literally see into the minds of wrongdoers, and what he has found there has left an indelible stain on his own mind. 'I put myself in his head. I become the horror.' For that reason he has joined the mysterious Millennium™ (how the hell can you trademark the word millennium?) a team of underground ex-law enforcement officers dedicated to hunting down evil in whatever shape or form it may take.

In the second series, Frank's wife is kidnapped, and he realises that all is not well within the group, and certain secrets have been kept from him, and he leaves. But the group has other ideas.

In series three, the group release a deadly virus cross country, leaving thousands dead in its wake. Feeling a bit pissed off, and afraid for his wife and daughter, Frank rejoins the FBI, where he teams up with a female agent, played irritatingly by Kirsten Cloke.

All fired up by the fear of the approaching new century, *Millennium™* was a great idea, but sadly ran out of steam, much like the millennium bug itself. Well worth catching for series 1 and 2, but the final one let it down.

Spookily, one of the directors was named David Nutter.

weblinks

www.imdb.com/title/tt0115270/
www.youtube.com/watch?v=fylS2x9JiVU
www.tv.com/millennium/show/1172/summary.html
en.wikipedia.org/wiki/Millennium_(TV_series)
www.amazon.co.uk/Millennium-1-3-DVD-Lance-Henriksen/dp/B0002W12XA/

OUT

UK – ITV (One Season)
Cast: Tom Bell *(Frank Ross)*, Norman Rodway *(Det Insp Bryce)*,
John Junkin *(Ralph Veneker)*, Brian Croucher *(Chris Cottle)*
Writer: Trevor Preston
Producers: Linda Agran, Johnny Goodman & Barry Hanson
First Broadcast (UK): 24 July 1978 – 28 August 1978
Runtime: 6 Episodes x 60 min
DVD: Network 2007

Frank Ross hits the street after eight years in prison, and finds the world a much changed place. He sees the streets full of punks and Arabs (the series was made in 1978 remember) and he heads home to his old house (strangely enough, a beautiful detached building just round the corner from my old school in Upper Tulse Hill) where he sets out to find whoever grassed him up all that time ago. During his search he explodes into ultra violence, not only with other villains, but also cops as bent as they are. As a matter of fact, on seeing it again I can understand where some of my own characters in my own books came from. Starring Tom Bell as Ross, looking as cadaverous as only he could, I'm not surprised that my old friend Derek Raymond aka Robin Cook wanted him for the unnamed Sergeant in the *Factory* novels, that were mooted to be made by BBC2 as a series, but never got off the ground, possibly because transferring his horrific vision of modern day London would send the good burghers into meltdown.

weblinks

www.imdb.com/title/tt0163476/
www.tv.com/out/show/17714/summary.html?q=out&tag=search_results;title;8
en.wikipedia.org/wiki/Out_%28miniseries%29
www.amazon.co.uk/Out-Complete-Special-Tom-Bell/dp/

THE PRISONER

UK – ITV (One Season)
Cast: Patrick McGoohan *(John Drake)*, George Markstein
(Man behind desk in title sequence), Angelo Muscat *(The Butler)*,
Peter Swanwick *(Supervisor)*
Writer: Patrick McGoohan
Producers: Patrick McGoohan & David Tomblin
First Broadcast (UK): 29 September 1967 – 1 February 1968
Runtime: 17 Episodes x 50 min
DVD:Network 2008

Used to watch this with the missus of the time, in black and white because we couldn't afford a colour telly, which somewhat spoiled the psychedelic effects, as a secret agent resigns from his job (usually assumed to be John Drake from *Danger Man**, but never made clear, like so much else in the series) and is then kidnapped and taken to The Village (Portmeirion, North Wales) a sort of home for retired spies, where he is given the number six as his identity. His catchphrase of the show: 'I am not a number! I am a free man'. McGoohan's character constantly tries to escape, and just as constantly is hauled back. What annoyed me about the show was that for a presumably intelligent man (he was in intelligence after all) our hero never put all the facts he learned about the whereabouts of the village together to help him get away, which was stupid. The hastily tacked together ending (there should have been thirty-six episodes, but Lew Grade refused to bankroll any more than seventeen, possibly because of the covert drug references) featured Alexis Kanner as a sort of spaced out hippy, and in the end there was no ending.

Be seeing you.

But hopefully not the 2009 version of the show, starring James Caviezel as Number Six. McGoohan must be spinning in his grave.

weblinks

www.imdb.com/title/tt0061287/
www.youtube.com/watch?v=om8Xwa3MhaU

www.tv.com/the-prisoner-uk/show/2867/summary.html
en.wikipedia.org/wiki/The_Prisoner
www.amazon.co.uk/Prisoner-DVD-Patrick-McGoohan/dp/

SURVIVORS

UK – BBC (Three Seasons)
Cast: Lucy Fleming *(Jenny Richards)*, Ian McMulloch *(Greg Preston)*,
Denis Lill *(Charles Vaughan)*, Stephen Dudley *(John Millon)*, Tanya Ronder
(Lizzie Willoughby), John Abineri *(Hubert Goss)*, Lorna Lewis *(Pet Simpson)*,
Carolyn Seymour *(Abby Grant)*
Writer: Terry Nation
Producer: Terence Dudley
First Broadcast (UK): 16 April 1975 – 8 June 1977
Runtime: 38 Episodes x 50 min
DVD: 2Entertain Video 2008

Yeah, I know there's been a recent remake, but for me *Survivors* will always
be a Nineteen Seventies phenomenon where it sat week after week reeking
of the decade that style forgot. Devised by Terry Nation, the premise was it
was the end of the world as we knew it, and no one felt in the least bit fine.
Especially the few (you guessed it) survivors who were immune to the virus
that decimated the entire population of the planet. Carolyn Seymour played
Abby Grant, constantly seeking her son Peter, aided by Greg Preston (Ian
McCulloch) the one man determined to reinstate civilisation, and anyone
else they pick up on the way.

Personally I could have done with more gunfire and less growing potatoes,
so I wrote my own version (*I Spied a Pale Horse* – Toxic Books) which I still
think is better.

weblinks

www.imdb.com/title/tt0072572/
www.youtube.com/watch?v=ePfyYIkntNE&feature=related
en.wikipedia.org/wiki/Survivors
www.tv.com/survivors-1975/show/9279/summary.html
www.amazon.co.uk/Survivors-1-3-Complete-Peter-Bowles/dp/

PAUL TEMPLE

UK – BBC (Four Seasons)
Cast: Francis Matthews *(Paul Temple)*, Ros Drinkwater *(Steve Temple)*
Writer: Francis Durbridge
Producer: Derrick Sherwin
First Broadcast (UK): 23 November 1969 – 1 September 1971
Runtime: 64 Episodes x 60 min
DVD: Acorn Media 2009

Now here's one to really get nostalgia fans' juices running. The character of Paul Temple was invented by writer Francis Durbridge in the 1930s as a crime-writing private investigator (funny how many of those turn up in crime fiction. A bit of wishful thinking I suspect), aided and abetted by his wife Steve. The novels were adapted, firstly for radio, then cinema and finally TV. Francis Matthews played Paul and Ros Drinkwater played Steve. In the books and radio plays, Temple was an urbane devil who swanned about in fast cars, wore stylish clothes, and Steve was very much a new woman getting involved up to her neck in most of the stories, which always involved cliff-hangers where someone (often Steve herself) was in deadly danger. But don't worry, with one bound they were free.

However, when transferred to TV, the format changed. Firstly, Durbridge himself was not writing the stories, they were not serials, as in the radio days, and the period was updated to the sixties. But Temple was just as suave, and Steve was just as likely to end up in trouble. Sadly, the original theme, *Coronation Scot*, was not used and replaced by original music by Ron Grainer.

weblinks

www.imdb.com/title/tt0159194/
www.tv.com/paul-temple/show/24633/summary.html
en.wikipedia.org/wiki/Paul_Temple#DVD_release
www.amazon.co.uk/Paul-Temple-DVD-Francis-Matthews/dp/B00264GB60/

BLUE HEELERS

AUSTRALIA – ITV (Thirteen Seasons)
Cast: Julie Nihill *(Christine 'Chris' Reilly)*, John Wood *(Sr Sgt Tom Croydon)*, Martin Sacks *(Sr. Det Patrick Joseph 'PJ' Hasham)*, Axl Taylor *(Len the Barman)*
Writers: Hal McElroy & Tony Morphett
Producer: Errol Sullivan
First Broadcast (AUS): 18 January 1994 – 4 June 2006
Runtime: 511 episodes x 60 min
DVD: Paramount Home Entertainment

The only non US/USA series in my list came across as a sort of mixture of *The Bill** and *A Country Practice*, set in Victoria, it became the most popular show in Australia, and was shown over here in fits and starts on afternoon and late evening time slots, often chopped into half-hour segments. Featuring a bunch of good-looking young cops in the fictional small town of Mount Thomas under the fatherly eye of Senior Sergeant Tom Croydon (John Wood). They look after everything from fencing disputes in the farmland to armed robbery and murder. The series was as comfortable as an old slipper but none the worse for that, but like an old slipper, around 2004, the show was showing the signs of age, and shedding viewers, so it became darker in character, the police station was destroyed by a bomb and Croydon's wife was kidnapped and raped. But nothing could save it, and after another two years it was killed off. After its cancellation most of the cast have turned up in *Sea Patrol,* which is like *Heelers* with heavily-armed destroyers. By God, those Ockers don't like anyone venturing close to their shores. Blue Heelers are particularly ugly dogs by the way, but none the worse for that.

weblinks

www.imdb.com/title/tt0108709/
www.youtube.com/watch?v=NvtjxoL_lfg
www.tv.com/blue-heelers/show/3333/summary.html
en.wikipedia.org/wiki/Blue_Heelers
www.amazon.co.uk/Blue-Heelers-Entire-Season-11-DVD/dp/

ROUTE 66

USA – ITV (Four Seasons)
Cast: Martin Milner *(Tod Stiles)*, George Maharis *(Buz Murdock)*,
Glenn Corbett *(Lincoln Case)*
Writer: Stirling Silliphant
Producers: Herbert B. Leonard & Sam Manners
Broadcast (US): 7 October 1960 – 13 March 1964
Runtime: 116 Episodes x 60 min in Black and White
DVD: Roxbury Entertainment 2008

Two cool cats, Martin Milner, playing Tod Stiles, and George Maharis playing Buz Murdock, take off for a road trip across America in a Chevrolet Corvette, living and loving along the way. Buz and Tod. Boy, did I want to be them. On the way they get involved with almost every contemporary social situation, from racism to feminism, and often ended up on the wrong side of the law. But justice always prevailed. George Maharis left the show in 1963 to become a pop star, but his solitary hit, *Teach Me Tonight*, only got to number 25 on the *Billboard* Top 100, so maybe that wasn't such a good idea. His place in the passenger seat was taken by Glenn Corbett as Lincoln Case.

weblinks

www.imdb.com/title/tt0053534/
www.youtube.com/watch?v=R_ykDw-06H8
www.tv.com/route-66/show/1044/summary.html
en.wikipedia.org/wiki/Route_66_%28TV_series%29
www.amazon.co.uk/Route-66-Season-Complete-Collection/dp/

NAKED CITY

USA – ITV (Four Seasons)
Cast: Harry Bellaver *(Det Frank Arcaro)*, Lawrence Dobkin *(Narrator)*,
Horace McMahon *(Lt. Michael 'Mike' Parker)*, Paul Burke *(Det Adam Flint)*
Writers: Stirling Silliphant & Howard Rodman
Producers: Herbert B. Leonard, Stanley Neufeld & Sam Manners
First Broadcast (US): 30 September 1958 to 29 May 1963

Runtime: 39 Episodes x 30 min & 99 Episodes x 60 min in Black and White

DVD: Image Entertainment 2005

'There are eight million stories in the naked city, and this is one of them'. So began every episode of this long running series set in New York and based on an Oscar winning 1948 film starring Barry Fitzgerald, and written by columnist Mark Hellinger. The camera roamed the city (the series was shot on location) as the cop heroes dug into the underbelly of Manhattan, sorting out the good from the bad, the quick from the dead.

Originally, the lead cop, Detective Lieutenant. Dan Muldoon (John McIntire) of the 65th Precinct taught his inexperienced partner Detective Jim Halloran (James Franciscus) the ways of the street, which were not always strictly by the book. Early on, Muldoon met his maker via a case of car vs petrol tanker. Messy! Halloran didn't last much longer and was written out after the first series. Enter Lieutenant Mike Parker (Horace McMahon), a real tough guy, and his new number two, Detective Adam Flint (Paul Burke).

Stars in waiting like Dustin Hoffman, Peter Falk and Robert Redford had small parts, however, the real star of the show was always New York itself. Shot in moody black and white, the camera had a long-running love affair with the town, from one end to the other, underlined by a superb score by Billy May.

Strange titles were always the thing too. Get these: *Today the Man Who Kills Ants is Coming, Howard Running Bear is a Turtle, The King of Venus Will Take Care of You.* They certainly don't name them like that anymore.

weblinks

www.imdb.com/title/tt0051297/
www.youtube.com/watch?v=YNRf7Dg0IMg&feature=related
www.tv.com/naked-city/show/4639/summary.html
en.wikipedia.org/wiki/Naked_City_%28TV_series%29
www.amazon.co.uk/Naked-City-Full-Region-NTSC/dp/

SPENSER: FOR HIRE

USA – BBC1 (Three Seasons)
Cast: Robert Urich *(Spenser)*, Avery Brooks *(Hawk)*,
Ron McLarty *(Sgt Frank Belson)*, Richard Jaeckel *(Lt. Martin Quirk)*,
Barbara Stock *(Susan Silverman)*
Writers: Robert B. Parker & John Wilder
Producer: William Robert Yates
First Broadcast (US): 20 September 1985 – 7 May 1988
Runtime: 66 Episodes x 60 min
DVD: Rykodisc 2005

OK, I know this is supposed to be the best of the genre, but I make the rules, and I've got to tell you that *Spenser: For Hire*, not to be confused with *Spender* starring Jimmy Nail, that was almost as bad, is one of the worst. And now I'll tell you why, more in sorrow than in anger. Robert B. Parker, now sadly deceased, started writing his Spenser novels in the early seventies. Brilliant stuff. In fact he made it seem so easy, I decided to have a bash myself in the mid-eighties, and it worked. OK again. So what do you do? Make the books into a TV show. Simple. Not so. The books are clever and witty. The TV shows not so. The books are extremely violent. The TV series not so. Anyway, to anyone who doesn't know. Spenser is a Boston-based private detective played by the late Robert Urich, not a million miles away from Raymond Chandler's Philip Marlowe (Spenser- Marlowe, geddit?).

He travels the streets of the city in a Ford Mustang, which I don't think he does in the books, and parks it inside his house (Robert Urich did the same thing in *Vegas*, where he also played a private eye, Dan Tanna. Does he have something about keeping his car next to his bed? Bit stinky I would have thought. I love my car, but I don't want it in my bedroom) and is assisted by Hawk (Avery Brooks) a bald-headed black, bad man, who actually does most of the violence in the novels. I think Parker was a bit squeamish and didn't want to make Spenser a cold-blooded killer which Hawk was. But not in the show. Also in the cast was Spenser's appalling girlfriend Susan Silverman (she's a bloody bore in the novels too) played by Barbara Stock. Brooks went on to have his own show (*A Man Called Hawk*), which was just as bad, if not worse

Do not watch these shows. Get the books instead!

LAW and ORDER (UK)

UK – BBC (One Season)
Cast: Peter Dean *(Jack Lynn)*, Derek Martin *(DI Fred Pyall)*,
Deirdre Costello *(Cathy Lynn)*, Billy Cornelius *(DS Eric Lethridge)*,
Alan Ford *(Clifford Harding)*, Ken Campbell *(Alex Gladwell)*,
Fred Haggerty *(DCI Tony Simmons)*
Writer: G.F. Newman
Producer: Tony Garnett
First Broadcast (UK): 6 April 1978 – 27 April 1978
Runtime: 4 episodes x 80min
DVD: 2Entertain Video 2008

Four films: four aspects of the British legal system in the 1970s; *A Detective's Tale*; *A Villain's Tale*; *A Brief's Tale*; *A Prisoner's Tale*. GF Newman wrote the scripts, the mighty Tony Garnett produced the series which starred Derek Martin as DI Fred Pyall, a hard-as-nails copper. The very same Derek Martin who is now the bumbling cabbie Charlie Slater, who's cab never seems to move, in *EastEnders*.

The show caused a hell of a ruckus at the time, the cops hated it, the lawyers hated it, politicians hated it, the press hated it. I rather liked it.

There is another *Law & Order UK*, a spin-off of the Dick Wolf franchise, which is so awful I have to leave the room if it comes on.

OUTRODUCTION / AFTERWORD

Whilst writing this book it's become obvious that one of the most important and long-lasting genres on TV is crime. It's like a basic need. Universal. The only other one to come close must be medical drama. Westerns had their time, but have mostly vanished from the mainstream, although now and then there's a renaissance promised, but it mostly fails. Then of course there's sci-fi, but really the monsters are just laughable. Not so in crime TV fiction. You can read about their monsters and worse every morning over the toast and marmalade. And still the shows keep on coming. So many that it's hard to keep up, especially when the satellite box goes on the blink. Here's just a few coming soon that will make this book almost redundant even before its published (only kidding). On this side of the Atlantic get ready to greet *The Accused* from the pen of Jimmy McGovern. A six-parter set in court. *The Silence*, where a young deaf girl who gets her hearing back and witnesses a brutal murder. *Aurelio Zen* from the books of Michael Dibden set in Rome. Peter Robinson's cop hero played by Stephen Tompkinson arrives in *DCI Banks: Aftermath*, Peter James' Detective Superintendent Roy Grace series is in pre-production and Sky are making a film featuring Mark Billingham's Detective Inspector Tom Thorne. Then from the USA comes one I haven't seen called *Castle* (but I've seen trailers, and oh boy it looks like it stinks on ice). In fact the only reason I mention it at all is because it features a handsome crime writer and a beautiful female cop on the trail of the bad guys together. Now how believable is that, as most of the male crime writers I know look like something the cat dragged in, ate, then sicked up again (present company excepted of course) and the females ain't much better believe me, no matter what photos they put on the covers of their books. New ones from over there for later this year, or next, include *Detroit187*, *The Whole Truth*, a remake of *HawaiiFive-0** (beware that one I think), *Blue Bloods*, *The Defenders** (Another remake I imagine), a *Criminal Minds** spin-off starring Forest Whitaker, *Outlaw*, *Law & Order: Los Angeles*, *Harry's Law*, and *Ride Along* from the makers of *The Shield**. Enough already. I know little about most of these at the moment. But what I do know is that some will die an early death, and some will survive possibly to become classics and feature in a book like this in twenty years' time. It's all part of the game. Anyway, there's bound to be something for every crime TV fan to enjoy somewhere in that lot.

ACKNOWLEDGEMENTS

Before I go, I must just make some acknowledgements, as no book like this can be done without help. Firstly, once again to Nick David, for real tight researching, and who will, all being well, be the father of twins before this book appears. And of course I wish his wife Gemma a safe and happy birth. Then there's Lucy Ramsey who spent hours on the Internet tracking down various obscure sites. Finally, apart from books previously mentioned in the text, to a greater or lesser extent, I used the publications on the next page for information. Once again, any mistakes are my own, or not, as the case might be.

That's all she wrote.

BIBLIOGRAPHY

The Penguin TV Companion
Third Edition – Jeff Evans Penguin Books 2006

The Ultimate TV Guide
Jon E. Lewis & Penny Stempel Orion Media 1999

The Lost Chronicles
Mark Cotta Vaz Channel 4 Books 2005

Secrets Of 24
Edited by Dan Burstein & Arne J. De Keizer Sterling Publishing 2007

Cracker: The Truth Behind the Fiction
John Crace Boxtree 1994

Between The Lines – Tony Clark's Dossier
Krystyna Zukowska Boxtree 1994

Spooks – The Personnel Files
No Author Credit (Must be top secret) Headline 2006

25 Years of Taggart
Thomas Quinn Headline 2007

The Billboard Book of USA Top 40 Hits (2nd Ed.)
Joel Whitburn Guinness Books 1985

Record Collector Rare Record Price Guide 2010

British Hit Singles & Albums Edition 17
Edited by David Roberts

Guinness World Records – 2004

INDEX OF TV CRIME SHOWS